This book belongs to

_____

...a woman blessed with
every spiriual blessing.

My Linise
EH 2022

Understanding Your Blessings in Christ

Elizabeth George

HARVEST HOUSE PUBLISHERS
EUGENE, OREGON

Cover design by Dugan Design Group, Bloomington, Minnesota

Cover photo © Wizdata / Wizdata, inc. / Alamy

Back cover author photo © Harry Langdon

Acknowledgments

As always, thank you to my dear husband, Jim George, M.Div., Th.M., for your able assistance, guidance, suggestions, and loving encouragement on this project.

UNDERSTANDING YOUR BLESSINGS IN CHRIST
Copyright © 2008 Elizabeth George
Published by Harvest House Publishers
Eugene, Oregon 97402
www.harvesthousepublishers.com

Library of Congress Cataloging-in-Publication Data
George, Elizabeth, 1944-
Understanding your blessings in Christ / Elizabeth George.
   p. cm.—(A woman after God's own heart)
ISBN 978-0-7369-1247-1 (pbk.)
ISBN 978-0-7369-3403-9 (eBook)
1. Bible. N.T. Ephesians—Textbooks. I. Title.
BS2695.55.G46 2008
227.' 50071—dc22

2008030535

Printed in the United States of America

18   19   20   / BP-SK /   13   12   11   10   9

Contents

Foreword

Before You Begin

Foreword

*F*or some time I have been looking for Bible studies that I could use each day that would increase my knowledge of God's Word. In my search, I found myself struggling between two extremes: Bible studies that required little time but also had little substance, or studies that were in-depth and demanded more time than I could give. I discovered that I wasn't alone—there were many other women like me who were busy yet desired to spend quality time studying God's Word.

That's why I became excited when Elizabeth George shared her desire to create a series of women's Bible studies that offered in-depth lessons that could be completed in just 15-20 minutes per day. When she completed the first study—on Philippians—I was eager to try it out. I had already studied Philippians many times, but this was the first time I had come to understand exactly how the whole book fit together and how it can truly be lived out in my life. Each lesson was simple but insightful—and was written especially to apply to me as a woman!

In the Woman After God's Own Heart® Bible study series, Elizabeth takes you step by step through the Scriptures, sharing wisdom she has gleaned from more than 20 years as a women's Bible teacher. The lessons are rich and meaningful because they're rooted in God's Word and have been lived out in Elizabeth's life. Her thoughtful and personable guidance makes you feel as though you are studying right alongside her—as if she is personally mentoring you in the greatest aspiration you could ever pursue: to become a woman after God's own heart.

If you're looking for Bible studies that can help you grow stronger in your knowledge of God's Word even in the most demanding of schedules, I know you'll find this series to be a welcome companion in your daily walk with God.

—LaRae Weikert
Vice President of Editorial,
Harvest House Publishers

Before You Begin

In my book *A Woman After God's Own Heart*®, I describe such a woman as one who ensures that God is first in her heart and the Ultimate Priority of her life. Then I share that one crucial way this desire can become reality is by nurturing a heart that abides in God's Word. To do so means that you and I must develop a root system anchored deep in God's Word.

Before you launch into this Bible study, take a moment to think about these aspects of a root system produced by the regular, faithful study of God's Word:

- *Roots are unseen*—You'll want to set aside time in solitude—"underground" if you will—to immerse yourself in God's Word and grow in Him.

- *Roots are for taking in*—Alone and with your Bible in hand, you'll want to take in and feed upon the truths of the Word of God and ensure your spiritual growth.

- *Roots are for storage*—As you form the habit of looking into God's Word, you'll find a vast, deep reservoir of divine hope and strength forming for the rough times.

- *Roots are for support*—Do you want to stand strong in the Lord? To stand firm against the pressures of life? The routine care of your roots through exposure to God's Word will cultivate you into a remarkable woman of endurance.[1]

I'm glad you've chosen this study out of my A Woman After God's Own Heart® Bible study series. My prayer for you is that the truths you find in God's Word through this study will further transform your life into the image of His dear Son and empower you to be the woman you seek to be: a woman after God's own heart.

In His love,

Elizabeth George

Opening God's Treasure Chest

y husband Jim, when teaching the Bible, often shares a story of a millionaire who was found dead in his squalid apartment...with money hidden and tucked away everywhere possible in his bare-bones home. He was a man who had riches galore, but failed to benefit from them or put them to use.

Sadly, many Christians live their daily lives as paupers when, in reality, they are princes and princesses in Christ. As you make your way through the New Testament epistle of Ephesians—referred to by one Bible scholar as "the Alps of the New Testament" and "Paul's third heaven epistle"[2]—pay special attention to the treasure of your riches in Christ.

Now, learn what Paul, the writer of this encouraging letter, has to say about himself and spiritual blessings in Christ.

9

Ephesians 1:1-2

¹ Paul, an apostle of Jesus Christ by the will of God, to the saints who are in Ephesus, and faithful in Christ Jesus:

² Grace to you and peace from God our Father and the Lord Jesus Christ.

Out of God's Word...

1. *Paul*—What does Paul say about himself in verse 1?

   And in Ephesians 3:1?

   Using an English dictionary, what is an *apostle?*

   How does Paul say he became an apostle (Ephesians 1:1)?

   What else do these scriptures tell you about Paul?

   Romans 1:1—

   Galatians 1:1—

   What these verses do not reveal is that Paul is writing from a prison in Rome, sometime between A.D. 60–62.[3]

2. *Paul's readers*—How does Paul describe his readers in verse 1?

Where are those he is writing to located?

What do you learn about Paul's ministry to these believers in Acts 20:31?

How widely was the message spread according to Acts 19:10?

According to Acts 19:19, what was the response among those who practiced magic?

Ephesus was the "flagship" of the churches of Asia Minor. Paul had planted the church. He had spent three years building up the church body, and later he had sent his young associate, Timothy, to pastor the church. Ephesians was not written to counteract any heresy or confront any specific problem. No, it was written to encourage his beloved friends. But being the teacher he was, Paul could not help reminding his friends how powerfully they had been equipped to experience the treasure of God's blessings in Christ.

3. *Paul's greeting*—What two riches and blessings does Paul point to as he greets his readers in verse 2?

   —

   —

What is the source of these remarkable spiritual blessings as stated in verse 2?

...and into Your Heart

- Paul was a "sent one," a messenger or delegate whose mission was to be God's representative. What do these verses teach you about your mission?

    Matthew 28:19-20—

    Acts 1:8—

    2 Corinthians 5:20—

- Note several ways you can send a more accurate and consistent message about Jesus to those closest to you.

- Paul referred to the Ephesian believers as "saints," as "set apart ones." They were not saints because they were dead. In fact, they were very much alive—alive in Christ! And they were not saints because of any merit of their own. No, they were described as saints because they were set apart by God to devote themselves to a holy and pure way of life. How can you better devote yourself to a holy and pure way of life? Jot down a list of ways to improve.

- Paul also referred to the Ephesian believers as "in Christ Jesus." He uses this phrase or a variation of it some ten times in the first 14 verses to stress our union with Christ. We have a relationship with God only because of Jesus Christ and only because we are "in" Him through belief and trust in Him. As believers we have *faith in Christ,* but we are also to be *faithful to Christ.* What changes must you make to enhance your reputation as one who is faithful to Christ?

- Paul concludes his introductory greeting with the claim that God, the Father, and Jesus together are offering grace and peace to believers in Christ. "Grace" means God's unmerited favor, and "peace" is what Jesus established between believers and God through His death on the cross. As a believer in Him you have peace in God *and* the peace of God. Read Ephesians 2:8 and comment on God's grace in your life.

- Now read John 14:27 and write a sentence or two about how you should live your life as a believer.

Heart Response

Paul had a deep love not only for Jesus Christ, but for the people in the body of Christ in Ephesus. The church there had weathered many trials and withstood the influences of a pagan society. Therefore Paul was eager to show his love for his readers and remind them of God's love and mercy for them as they stood firm against the worldly pressures that surrounded them. Because of their relationship with God through Christ, Paul wrote to encourage them by reminding them of the riches and blessings that were theirs as believers.

Allow Paul's salutation to the Ephesians to bring grace and peace to your heart as you acknowledge your blessings in Christ. Don't fail to enjoy the treasure to be found in God's Word. Count on it! Look to it! Trust in it! When you do, your life will be transformed, others will notice, and, most important of all, God will be honored.

Praising God's Plan

Ephesians 1:3-6

I'm sure you've had the experience of talking with people who seem to suffer from a low self-image or have a "poor me" attitude. Over time I've learned that when I, like them, am tempted to give in to such thinking, I have a sure remedy. That remedy is found in this lesson about Paul's words to the hearts of his friends…and to you and me. Read them now.

Ephesians 1:3-6

3 Blessed be the God and Father of our Lord Jesus Christ, who has blessed us with every spiritual blessing in the heavenly places in Christ,

4 just as He chose us in Him before the foundation of the world, that we should be holy and without blame before Him in love,

> [5] having predestined us to adoption as sons by Jesus Christ to Himself, according to the good pleasure of His will,
>
> [6] to the praise and glory of His grace, by which He made us accepted in the Beloved.

Out of God's Word...

1. *God*—As you look at the verses above—the beginning of a very l-o-n-g list of praises to God for what He's accomplished for believers in Christ—what is said about God and what He has done?

   Verse 3— *Every Spiritual blessings*

   Verse 4— *He chose us so we should stay Holy before*

   Verse 5— *by the pleasure of His will*

   Verse 6— *praise + glory to God because He made us acceptable to Him*

   Just a few notes: The concept that God "chose us" is not based on any merit or influence on our part. Even before time began, it was God's desire to select individuals or groups for specific purposes. This practice became specific with Abraham and his descendants (Genesis 12:1-3) and can be traced down through time to those who today make up Christ's body, the church. Also Paul uses the term "adoption" to refer to those predestined or marked out beforehand by God to become His children through a process Paul compares to adoption.

2. *God's blessings*—Circle the personal pronouns "us" and "we" in verses 3-6 on pages 15-16. Then list the specific blessings God causes His people to enjoy.

   love God & our fellow people

3. *God's plans and purposes*—As you look again at verses 3-6, note the *when, where, how,* and *why* of God's plans and purposes in what He has done for you and in blessing you.

   When— *1960's?*

   Where— *Colorado*

   How— *By being included & loved by fellow church people*

   Why— *Because of their love for Christ & other people*

...*and into Your Heart*

- *The scope of God's blessings*—Think about the scope of God's blessings to you—that you have been crowned with every spiritual blessing in Christ! How can and should you acknowledge this unbelievable resource that is yours? *By believing & showing respect for other people*

How should the knowledge of God's blessings cause you to think and live? *I needed to believe first of His love for everyone*

• *The sphere of God's blessings*—Ephesus was a wealthy city and the location of the temple of Diana, considered to be one of the wonders of the ancient world. However, even those who lived in such a city needed more in life. Jot down here the sphere of God's blessings as stated in verse 3. *We are blessed with every spiritual blessing*

When Paul uses the phrase "in the heavenly places," he is pointing out that the blessings mentioned in Ephesians 1:3-6 are spiritual and not material, eternal and not of this world. As you think about the scope and sphere of these "heavenly" blessings, how do they compare to the earthly and worldly material benefits most people consider to be important in daily life?

What warning and advice does 1 John 2:15-17 give concerning wealth and the world in...

...verse 15?

...verse 16?

...verse 17?

According to Colossians 3:1-2, what are you to set and not set your mind, heart, and desires on while you await heaven?

- *The source of God's blessings*—In one word, what is the source of God's many spiritual blessings (verse 6)?

  acceptable

As a child of God, you have the benefit of knowing God. You also have everything you need to grow spiritually. As you think about your vast spiritual wealth in Christ as recorded in a mere four verses, what should be your...

...spiritual response? *love & thinking*

...mental response? *remember*

...practical response? *use what the Bible says to do - Love one another*

Heart Response

Surely God's message to your heart is calling you to stop and marvel at what God has done for you through and in His Son, Jesus Christ. Think about the list of riches God has bestowed on you which are recorded in these very few verses:

- God has blessed you...with every spiritual blessing...in the heavenly places...in Christ.

- God chose you in Christ...before the foundation of the world...to be holy and without blame before Him...in love.

- God predestined you...to adoption as sons...by Jesus Christ to Himself...according to the good pleasure of His will.

How fortunate you are! You were lost and without hope, but God in His great mercy forgave your sins through His Son's death on your behalf. Then, wonder of wonders, you were taken into God's own family and given the status of a daughter or son. Pause and reflect on why this lesson is a cure for any Christian, including you, who might entertain a low self-image or "poor me" attitude. Offer praise to God for His plan for you. Purpose to devote yourself to fulfilling His purposes. Show the world your true identity as His child—"to the praise of the glory of His grace."

*L*esson 3

Realizing God's Will

*P*erhaps because our family lived in Southern California for 30-plus years, I dearly love the ocean. Amazingly, every time I read the verses spotlighted in this lesson, I think of the Pacific Ocean. I recall the many times I reveled in the sight and sound of its surf and the incessant repetition of splashing, crashing, sloshing-up-on-the-shore waves, only to be followed by another...and another...and another.

The two previous lessons in Ephesians have been like the breakers of a surf. Each Scripture passage was powerful, thrilling, and breathtaking, so spectacular I could hardly expect another to be as exhilarating. And yet the blessings God delights in bestowing upon His people in and through His Son just keep on rolling in. Revel in them with me once again!

21

Ephesians 1:7-10

⁷ In Him we have redemption through His blood, the forgiveness of sins, according to the riches of His grace

⁸ which He made to abound toward us in all wisdom and prudence,

⁹ having made known to us the mystery of His will, according to His good pleasure which He purposed in Himself,

¹⁰ that in the dispensation of the fullness of the times He might gather together in one all things in Christ, both which are in heaven and which are on earth—in Him.

Out of God's Word...

1. *Christ's limitless gift to us* (verses 7-8)—List the believer's benefits in Christ as seen in...

   ...verse 7— *redemption thru His blood*

   ...verse 8— *thru His wisdom & prudence*

Slaves in Paul's day were bought and sold like cattle or furniture. Paul's use of the word "redemption" means to purchase in the slave market and set free. What do these verses say about your redemption?

Galatians 3:13—

Galatians 5:1— *He followed scripture written Stand fast*

Colossians 1:13-14— *Redemtion thru Christ*

1 Peter 1:18-19— *Saved by Christs death & rise from all*

The primary result of redemption is forgiveness. Through the shedding of His blood, Jesus Christ actually took the sins of the world and carried them far, far away, never to return again. How was your forgiveness achieved (Ephesians 1:7)? *Thru Christs Blood*

2. *The Father's limitless purpose for us* (verses 9-10)—Verse 9 describes God's purpose. How does Paul describe or refer to God's revealed plan before it was made known?
In His time bring everything together

What reason is given for God's revealing of His plan?
In Gods time not ours

Verse 10 details God's purpose and will. What do you learn about the purpose of God's redemption?
In His time every thing will come together in Christ

What is the extent of God's plan?
For Completion & all in Heaven with Him

...and into Your Heart

- "According to the riches of His grace" describes the extent of God's redemption and forgiveness. If Paul had written "*out of* the riches of His grace," a limitation of God's grace could be involved. However, by writing "*according to* the riches," Paul expresses God's infinite and eternal redemption and forgiveness based on infinite and eternal grace. What do these scriptures add to your understanding of forgiveness?

Psalm 103:12— *As far as east from west*

John 1:29— *He saw Jesus coming + said forgiven to every person of God*

Hebrews 9:26— *Jesus died for all who believe —*

How should the reality and blessing of God's forgiveness influence the way you live and think each day? Are there any changes you should make? *Be more forgiving*

pray for forgiveness

- The effects of redemption are "wisdom and prudence." When a person becomes a believer in Christ, God lavishly gives him or her the ability to discern the right actions to take in any given situation. Note what these scriptures say about the wisdom and insight that come from God:

Proverbs 9:10— *understanding*

Matthew 11:25— *Gods hid His pleasure to children first*

1 Corinthians 2:12— *we can understand because of Gods Holy Spirit*

1 Corinthians 2:16— *Only the spirit can understand*

James 1:5— *ask for wisdom from God & He gives it*

List some ways you can tap into God's wisdom today.

pray & surrender to God
Special understanding

• What further insight can be gained about the extent of God's plan from:

Philippians 2:10-11— *at the name of Jesus - be exalted*

Colossians 1:19-20— *Lordship is universal*

Your life is not hapless and purposeless. God has a plan for every step of your way! How does this truth comfort you? Encourage you? Empower you?

- "Dispensation" (verse 10) refers to the management of a household or estate. You've probably experienced managing a household, making a master plan, and creating a time line for achieving or finishing a project. God is the Master Manager, and He is organizing everything according to His timing, which will culminate when everything in heaven and on earth is united under Christ's headship and authority. How does the knowledge of God's perfect administration of your life and His plan for all things help you with today's challenges?

Heart Response

Whenever your life seems to be out of control or you feel like the world is crashing in on you, realize God is sovereign. He is in charge, and He is a faithful, flawless administrator. He is working out His good and acceptable and perfect will. His purpose in saving you and showering a continuing multitude of blessings upon you has been established. Your future is secure in Him due to the riches of His grace. God's blessings are yours! Your heart- and soul-response to God's plan of redemption for you should always and forever be one of reveling in the truth and giving unending praise and thanksgiving to Him for all He has and will give you "according to the riches of His grace."

Counting on God's Inheritance

Ephesians 1:11-14

My parents were both schoolteachers who worked hard all their lives. After years of teaching they both retired and followed a mutual passion of buying, restoring, and selling antiques. With their retirement incomes and their antique hobby they managed to accumulate enough funds to provide me and my three brothers with a small inheritance, which my husband and I used to help pay down our home mortgage. Every day as I walk through my home I can't help but think of my dear, sweet parents and their gift to me and my family.

Maybe you won't have an inheritance from an earthly father, but take heart! Your heavenly Father has given you a heavenly inheritance that you can count on.

Ephesians 1:11-14

¹¹ In Him also we have obtained an inheritance, being predestined according to the purpose of Him who works all things according to the counsel of His will,

¹² that we who first trusted in Christ should be to the praise of His glory.

¹³ In Him you also trusted, after you heard the word of truth, the gospel of your salvation; in whom also, having believed, you were sealed with the Holy Spirit of promise,

¹⁴ who is the guarantee of our inheritance until the redemption of the purchased possession, to the praise of His glory.

Out of God's Word...

Prior to verse 11, Paul addresses both Jews and Gentiles in the city of Ephesus. Now in verses 11-14 he makes a distinction in the background and blessings of three groups.

1. What pronoun does Paul use for himself and other Jews who believed in Christ (verses 11-12)?

    we - you

    What pronoun does he use for the Gentiles who believed (verse 13)?   *you*

    What pronoun does he use for both groups (verse 14)?

    our

2. This passage is about what Christ has accomplished for all believers. Note here from verses 11-12 the many blessings He provided for those who belong to Him who had a Jewish background, including Paul.

   predestined inheritance - eternal life in Heaven

3. It is truly amazing what Christ has done for Jewish believers, but what about the Gentiles? Jot down from verse 13 the major blessing enjoyed by Gentiles and believers today. *We are promised salvation*

   How is the Holy Spirit a blessing for both groups of believers—both Jews and Gentiles—while they wait for their future inheritance? *genuine our faith is has our guarantee*

4. What do you learn about the Holy Spirit in...

   ...verse 13? *proof*

   ...verse 14? *guarantee of salvation*

5. Now look at verse 13. What is said about...

   ..."the word"? *of truth the gospel of salvation*

   ..."the gospel"?

6. How do both verses 11-12 and 13-14 end?

we need to give God our glory

....and into Your Heart

- Describe again "the mystery" referred to in verse 9.

Recognition to God

In a few words, what explanation of that mystery do you now discover in verses 11-14?

Our interdance from God

- *Your life in Christ*—What truths in verses 13-14 cause you to reevaluate your life as a Christian?

talk to God

Your attachment to the world—How should these truths—these many blessings—alter your attachment to the things of this world?

Your mission to others—You heard the good news and responded! Now it's your turn to reach out to others. What will you do today to share the gospel of Christ with others? Any specific people in mind?

- What does 1 Peter 1:1-4 say about your wonderful inheritance? *grace to you + God glorified*

- How are you to acknowledge God's gracious acts according to Ephesians 1:12 and 14? *praise + glory trust in God*

  How are you doing this on a daily basis, or how can you make it a daily habit?

Heart Response

Think on it—As a believer in Jesus Christ and one who trusts in Him, you've been given an inheritance in Him that is sealed and guaranteed by the Holy Spirit.

Mark it well—Believers are not saved and blessed for their own glory, but for God's. "The design of redemption is to exhibit the grace of God in such a conspicuous manner as to fill all hearts with wonder and all lips with praise."[4]

Give praise for it—Paul was in the habit of praising. In Ephesians 1:6 he praised God. In verse 12 he praised Jesus Christ. And here he informs us that the Holy Spirit's work will be to the praise of God's glory. Give God the heart response of praise. Make it your habit, for praising God is one thing you do on earth that you will continue to do in heaven. Praise God from whom all blessings flow!

practice here praise here so we will be ready! Amazing

*L*esson 5

Praying for Spiritual Insight
Ephesians 1:15-23

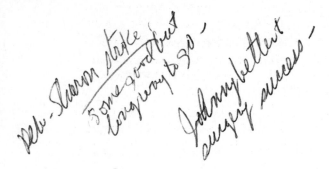

When you love someone, you can't help but pray for them. That's because you carry them in your heart everywhere you go. And if your friends are far away and you're unable to express your love and support to them personally, you can pray. Jesus prayed for His disciples in John 17. Paul prayed for the Philippian believers in Philippians 1, the Christians in Colosse in Colossians 1, and now for his friends in Ephesus. As you examine Paul's passionate prayer that follows, notice his habit of giving thanks to God for his friends and praying for them to develop spiritual eyes for their increased spiritual insight.

Ephesians 1:15-23

¹⁵ Therefore I also, after I heard of your faith in the Lord Jesus and your love for all the saints,

¹⁶ do not cease to give thanks for you, making mention of you in my prayers:

¹⁷ that the God of our Lord Jesus Christ, the Father of glory, may give to you the spirit of wisdom and revelation in the knowledge of Him,

¹⁸ the eyes of your understanding being enlightened; that you may know what is the hope of His calling, what are the riches of the glory of His inheritance in the saints,

¹⁹ and what is the exceeding greatness of His power toward us who believe, according to the working of His mighty power

²⁰ which He worked in Christ when He raised Him from the dead and seated Him at His right hand in the heavenly places,

²¹ far above all principality and power and might and dominion, and every name that is named, not only in this age but also in that which is to come.

²² And He put all things under His feet, and gave Him to be head over all things to the church,

²³ which is His body, the fullness of Him who fills all in all.

Out of God's Word...

1. *Paul praises God for his friends* (verses 15-16)—What had Paul heard about the Christians in Ephesus?

They loved Jesus + wanted to share it

What effect did this information have on Paul?

asked them to continue to pray for him

2. *Paul prays for the believers* (verses 17-19)—Paul did not ask God for anything physical or material for his friends, but rather asked that their spiritual eyes be opened, that they might recognize the spiritual blessings they already possessed. Make a list of Paul's specific requests for his friends and fellow believers.

They continue to be thankful for Jesus
Continue to pray for him + each other

3. *Paul points to the power of God* (verses 19-22)—List what God's power achieved. *Put every person/thing under Jesus because of love*

God's power is so tremendous that Paul uses four different dynamic words to get his point across:

- *power*—meaning capability. Our word *dynamite* comes from this word.

- *working*—meaning effective activity. Our word *energy* comes from this word.

- *mighty*—meaning a force that overcomes resistance. This word is used only of God's capabilities.

- *power*—meaning bodily or muscular strength.

Taken together, these four words describe God's all-inclusive strength and power.

4. *Paul praises Christ* (verses 22-23)—Paul introduces the church. How is the church described? *The Church*

is the people & make up the body of Christ

To what extent does Christ indwell the church?

By love & caring

...and into Your Heart

- Note here how Paul described the Ephesian Christians in verse 15. *love of Church & all saints*

  How do you compare with the believers in Ephesus— with their faith, love, and impact on others?

  good but always try to work more on prayer for others

- List at least two lessons you've learned about prayer and the emphasis of your prayers and concerns for fellow believers from Ephesians 1:15-23.

  Need to always pray about all circumstance and love all people

  —

• What struck you most as you read about God's power and Christ's supremacy? Was anything new to you? Did your thinking about God or confidence in Him change, and if so, in what ways?

Heart Response

As we close Ephesians chapter 1, realize that Paul is a prisoner. He has already spent two years in prison in Caesarea (Acts 24:27). Now he will spend more years in jail (Acts 28:30).What can a prisoner do, especially an innocent one? The options are many: rant, rave, blame others, question God, resent his past service and faithfulness, sink into depression, regret the passion that earned his imprisonment for the cause of Christ, wish he had been less outspoken...

But no, not Paul. Paul praised! He gushed! He effervesced! His outbursts of worship and lists of blessings are numerous and run throughout this entire epistle. The overflow of Paul's heart is evidence that he meditated on God's sovereign plan, His solemn pledge, the Spirit's indwelling and activity, the Son's supremacy, and the shining effects of God's grace.

Paul also prayed...that he and his fellow believers—and you!—would develop "spiritual eyes" for seeing and understanding our spiritual riches and blessings in Jesus Christ, that we would...

• grow to know God better,

- look with great hope and anticipation to His upward calling,

- understand our special relationship as His own inheritance, and

- experience God's power moment by moment in our lives.

In addition, Paul penned this letter, pouring out his heart to encourage others, while he himself was incarcerated. Paul may have been locked up, but his heart was not!

What are your difficult circumstances today? Praise God and pray for spiritual eyes to see and understand the spiritual riches and blessings that are yours in Jesus Christ no matter what your circumstances. Do as Paul did and pen a few words of hope, comfort, and strength to someone else. And pray—for yourself, for others, and for the church.

Lesson 6

Coming Alive in Christ

Ephesians 2:1-10

*H*ave you noticed how *l-o-n-g* Paul's sentences are as he reaches for words to describe God's work in His people's lives and His many marvelous blessings? God's blessings are literally heaped upon His people...and Paul's words seem to be heaped upon themselves as he conveys them. Dive in again and luxuriate in the inspired apostle's expression of new incredible truths about what it means to be alive in Christ.

Ephesians 2:1-10

[1] And you He made alive, who were dead in trespasses and sins,

[2] in which you once walked according to the course of this world, according to the prince of

the power of the air, the spirit who now works in the sons of disobedience,

³ among whom also we all once conducted ourselves in the lusts of our flesh, fulfilling the desires of the flesh and of the mind, and were by nature children of wrath, just as the others.

⁴ But God, who is rich in mercy, because of His great love with which He loved us,

⁵ even when we were dead in trespasses, made us alive together with Christ (by grace you have been saved),

⁶ and raised us up together, and made us sit together in the heavenly places in Christ Jesus,

⁷ that in the ages to come He might show the exceeding riches of His grace in His kindness toward us in Christ Jesus.

⁸ For by grace you have been saved through faith, and that not of yourselves; it is the gift of God,

⁹ not of works, lest anyone should boast.

¹⁰ For we are His workmanship, created in Christ Jesus for good works, which God prepared beforehand that we should walk in them.

Out of God's Word...

1. *God's estimation of man without Christ* (verses 1-3)—List here the appalling condition of the man or woman who is not in Christ. Keep in mind that this is a description of you before you believed in Christ.

   walked in tres passes + Sin + didn't Know the Lord Jesus

2. *God's great mercy in Christ* (verses 4-7)—Now read verses 4-6. What are the first two words?

    Show mercy

    How is God described in verse 4? *His great love for his people on earth*

    What did God accomplish for us according to verses 5-6?

    — *By Gods grace*

    — *His love for us*

    — *promises us heaven*

    What is the final statement made in verse 5?

    Saved by grace

    Why has God in His great grace bestowed such rich blessings upon us (verse 7)?

    Kindness toward us

3. *God's great purpose for us in Christ* (verses 8-10)—How is salvation described in verses 8-9?

    Saved thru grace to share Jesus with others

    What words are repeated in verses 5 and 8? *Saved by grace in Jesus*

    What is a part of God's purpose in our salvation, and when was it determined (verse 10)? *prepares us before we have a salvation to walk thru with Christ*

.....*and into Your Heart*

- Review the Scripture passage again, considering the contrast between man's natural condition and his spiritual position as one who is alive in Christ. As you read, note here what you have been saved from. *eternal life*

  away from God

  Now note what you have been saved for.

  To love, teach + learn

  Who took the initiative to save you from the consequences of your sin, and why? *My Mother + grand Mother when I was born*

- Considering your previous separation from God, how should your new life in Christ affect...

  ...your attitude toward the lost? *talk to them about Jesus + why we need to love Him*

  ...your responsibility to help and serve others? *Bible study, Sunday School class + Church*

  ...your love for God and your appreciation for His love for you? *Thankful*

• How does your life today differ from your life before Christ? Share a few instances of change. Then note any additional changes that need to be made.

Should love all relatives even if some are BRATS !

Heart Response

"Mirror, mirror, on the wall…" What woman isn't familiar with these words? And what woman doesn't spend some portion of her day in front of a mirror? Sound familiar?

But in this passage, God uses Paul to cause us to see ourselves as God sees us. We must never lose sight of what God has done for us, of our identity in His Son's life, death, resurrection, and ascension into heaven.

Think about it! Before you were in Christ you were:

• Christless—"without Christ"

• homeless—"alienated"

• messageless—"strangers from the covenants of promise"

• hopeless—"having no hope," and

• godless—"without God in the world."[5]

"But God, who is rich in mercy, because of His great love with which He loved us" (verse 4) changed all this.

Seeking to express his heart of gratitude to God for salvation, John Newton wrote these words in the hymn *Amazing Grace:* "I once was lost, but now am found, was blind, but now I see." How will you pour out your gratitude and thanksgiving to God for the new life you have in Christ?

Breaking Down Barriers

Ephesians 2:11-18

*P*eace is something people not only want but need. We seek peace, march for peace, pray for peace, even go to war for peace! However, Jesus Christ is the way to peace and the source of peace for every person. And, as you will see in the verses that follow, Christ is also the way and the source of peace among all believers in the body of Christ. Each Christian comes from a different background, upbringing, lineage, and environment. But in Christ we are unified.

As Paul addresses the subject of peace, you will notice names and labels given to various groups of people. You'll also notice that the groups were similar in their sin and lostness. But, blessing upon blessings, you will also witness the Savior magnificently removing all barriers and joining all believers not only to Himself, but to each other.

Ephesians 2:11-18

[11] Therefore remember that you, once Gentiles in the flesh—who are called Uncircumcision by what is called the Circumcision made in the flesh by hands—

[12] that at that time you were without Christ, being aliens from the commonwealth of Israel and strangers from the covenants of promise, having no hope and without God in the world.

[13] But now in Christ Jesus you who once were far off have been brought near by the blood of Christ.

[14] For He Himself is our peace, who has made both one, and has broken down the middle wall of separation,

[15] having abolished in His flesh the enmity, that is, the law of commandments contained in ordinances, so as to create in Himself one new man from the two, thus making peace,

[16] and that He might reconcile them both to God in one body through the cross, thereby putting to death the enmity.

[17] And He came and preached peace to you who were afar off and to those who were near.

[18] For through Him we both have access by one Spirit to the Father.

Out of God's Word...

1. List the terms and phrases used to describe the general condition of those "without Christ" in verses 11-12.

It helps to realize that before the coming of Jesus Christ, Gentiles and Jews shunned each other. Jews considered Gentiles unfit to have a relationship with God. And the Gentiles hated the Jews for their claims of superiority due to their heritage. Christ, however, revealed the complete sinfulness of *both* Jew and Gentile. In grace, He offered His salvation to *both*. Only Christ could, can, and does break down all walls of division, pride, and prejudice. Also, only Christ could, can, and does reconcile believers to God and unify them in one body.

2. Note from verse 13 the great change that occurred in those without Christ and the means by which their condition changed. *long way from lost Christ*

3. A "wall of partition," or a "hatred-barrier,"[6] existed between the Jews and Gentiles. Read verses 14-16. According to verse 14, how did Christ accomplish peace between the Gentiles and the Jews? *Christ is peace conecting the division*

   What was achieved by Christ in verse 15?

   He abolished *the old testament laws*

   He created *one man from*

   He produced *came + gave peace for all*

   What was the purpose of Christ's sacrifice according to verse 16? *Bring to reconcile with God thru Him*

4. What was Jesus' peace mission as described in verses 17-18? *left us with Holy Spirit of God*

...and into Your Heart

- Look up the word "enmity" (verse 15) in a dictionary and write out the definition here.

Hostility hatred ill will malignant disposition

- When Paul spoke of "the middle wall of separation," he was referring to the literal wall in the Temple that separated Jews from Gentile converts while worshiping God. Paul explains that Christ abolished not only the physical wall in the Temple, but also the ceremonial laws, feasts, and sacrifices that separated Jews from Gentiles. What Christ accomplished for those in Ephesus was also accomplished for you and all believers. How should Christ's removal of *all* barriers affect your view, opinion, and respect of all other Christians, regardless of race, wealth, social standing, family ties, etc.?

accept them for what they are — I don't have to have anything to do with them

- What do these scriptures say about unity in the body of Christ?

    Romans 10:12-13— *Everyone who calls on the Lord will be saved*

    Galatians 3:28— *Everyone is one in Christ*

- Can you think of several changes that need to occur in your thinking, your speech, your actions toward other Christians that will promote "the unity of the Spirit in the bond of peace" (Ephesians 4:3)? Note them now and make them real in your life.

—

—

• Peace like a river! Who doesn't need peace? What do you learn about Christ and His peace in these verses?

Isaiah 9:6—

John 14:27— *He leaves us with peace d do not be afraid*

John 16:33— *Speak clearly & He warns to expect worldly trouble – But He will be with me*

• What stressful or threatening situation is robbing you of God's peace? How will you tap into the knowledge that Christ "Himself is our peace" (Ephesians 2:14)?

Remember Jesus is with me – however a situation goes

Heart Response

Jim and I have some incredible neighbors, a husband and wife who both serve their country through the military. In recent years, one was deployed to Iraq and the other to Afghanistan with the goal of bringing peace to those countries. When their tours of duty were complete, however, instead of coming home, their units remained because the goal of peace had not been achieved. To this day, as of this writing, peace is still not a reality.

History reveals that most peace missions fail. But the peace achieved by the blood of Christ is real and eternal. I hope you have grasped the peace our Savior accomplished between you and God, and between you and all believers, no matter their race or origin.

What wells up in your heart and soul as you recall the moment when the barrier between you and God was removed? And what would you like to say to God in thanksgiving? As Paul wrote, you were once far off from the Father, but have now been brought near to Him (verse 13). And the same is true of all those in the body of Christ.

Thank you for a neighbor that asked me to go to Church with Her - Hadn't gone for about 1 year, traveled most weekends for our racing horses - found lifelong friend & believe (the best & longest was our pastor at time & wife Jean - They stopped this fall Hadn't seen them for years it was a joyful reunion - also the person I worked with in Co. Womens was here & we reconnected - what a joy!!

Being a Member of God's Household

Ephesians 2:19-22

*A*s a writer I've learned that a metaphor is a powerful tool in written communication. A *metaphor* is a word or phrase used symbolically to refer to or describe something else. When a writer wants to help a reader grasp an idea or concept, a metaphor or word picture is effective.

As Paul seeks to describe what it means to be in Christ, he utilizes the common and familiar illustration—a metaphor—of a building or house. As you study the scriptures spotlighted in this lesson, note what you learn about God's household, its foundation, cornerstone, ultimate completion, purpose, and those who live within it—the "members" of the household of God. As you complete this lesson, keep in mind the book of Ephesians is about understanding the blessings of being a member of the church, the body of

Christ, and the unity you enjoy with other Christians—other members of the household of God.

Have fun with these verses. And don't forget to notice the metaphors!

Ephesians 2:19-22

¹⁹ Now, therefore, you are no longer strangers and foreigners, but fellow citizens with the saints and members of the household of God,

²⁰ having been built on the foundation of the apostles and prophets, Jesus Christ Himself being the chief cornerstone,

²¹ in whom the whole building, being fitted together, grows into a holy temple in the Lord,

²² in whom you also are being built together for a dwelling place of God in the Spirit.

Out of God's Word...

1. Read verse 19. Before a person is in Christ, how is he or she described? *stranger to Christ*
   don't know how it feels till they do
   "the inner peace)

   —

   How are those in Christ described? *fellow citizens*
   — in Christ we believe in Him

   —

What additional information does Philippians 3:20 add to this description? *Able to do more than we knew Before al accept Christ*

2. Now read verse 20. How is "the household of God" described? *Church of Christ Believers*

And how is Christ described? *He is forever*

What information does 1 Peter 2:6 add to this description of Christ? *Cornerstone*

3. What becomes of "the household of God" as revealed in verses 21-22? *We should follow in His foot steps C what ever he wants us to do -*

Verse 21— *Because He suffered for me*

Verse 22— *He was perfect - Comitted nosin & no decuit was He didn't talk*

What additional information do you learn about the members of God's household in 1 Peter 2:5? *accepting sacrifices in my life so sl will put my faith in Jesus -*

.....and into Your Heart

- Look again at this passage of Scripture and fill in the blanks to picture the "house" or "building" Paul is describing.

  The foundation is _Christ_

  The cornerstone is _Christ_

  The building is growing into _a Church_

  The stones in the building are _us?_

  The occupant of the building is _Christ + believers_

  How does this picture enhance your understanding of the church, the body of Christ? _Remember all people can be accepted to Christ and our Church doors are open_

  Where and how do you see yourself fitting into this household? _faithful + be support for other believers_

- The foundational role of the apostles and prophets was to direct attention to Christ as the only true Savior. What will you do today to direct the attention of others to Christ as Savior?

- Not only are you a member of the household or family of God, but you are "a dwelling place of God in the Spirit" (verse 22). Where did God "dwell" in Exodus 25:8?

In Exodus 40:34-38? *a cloud they were to follow*

In 1 Kings 8:1-11? *Moved the ark to solomon*

God no longer dwells in man-made temples, nor does He dwell in church buildings. Where does He dwell today according to...

...1 Corinthians 6:19-20? (Also note your responsibility.) *In hearts of believers & I need to show respect and talk to all people*

...Ephesians 2:20-22? *When I believed I felt a special feeling in my soul*

Heart Response

As I think through these few verses that show us so much about life in Christ and our place in His household, I am praying for three heart responses from my own heart...and from your heart as well.

First, I must be faithful and fervent to share the truth about Christ as Savior with those who are still strangers and foreigners to the kingdom of God. God is still building His household, and new members are continually being added.

Second, I must guard against any prejudice in my heart as a member of the body of Christ and the family of God. The cross of Christ makes all believers equal—young and old, male and female, Jew and Gentile, rich and poor, and black, white, and every other color of skin from all the nations! All who are believers belong to Christ, dwell in the household of God, and share in every spiritual blessing in Christ.

And third, as a believer in Christ, I am a dwelling—a temple—in which God lives by His Spirit. This is a staggering thought! Therefore I must take care to do as Paul said—to glorify God in my body and in my spirit, which are God's (1 Corinthians 6:19-20).

He lives in me by Spirit + I need to show this in my daily life—

> The church is never a place,
> but always a people; never a fold,
> but always a flock; never a sacred building,
> but always a believing assembly.[7]
>
> —JOHN HAVLIK

*L*esson 9

Discovering the Mystery

Ephesians 3:1-13

*E*veryone loves a mystery. And there's no doubt that there are many mysteries surrounding God, His character, and the knowledge of Him. He is indeed unfathomable and un-understandable. As the Bible says, "The secret things belong to the LORD our God" (Deuteronomy 29:29). But there are also certain "things"—mysteries—that were hidden until New Testament times, when God chose to reveal them.

One of the great truths in the epistle to the Ephesians is the "mystery" of the church. In the verses that follow, Paul explains the mystery—that Gentile believers are now united with Jewish believers in one new body (Ephesians 3:6).

Ephesians 3:1-13

[1] For this reason I, Paul, the prisoner of Christ Jesus for you Gentiles—

[2] if indeed you have heard of the dispensation of the grace of God which was given to me for you,

[3] how that by revelation He made known to me the mystery (as I have briefly written already,

[4] by which, when you read, you may understand my knowledge in the mystery of Christ),

[5] which in other ages was not made known to the sons of men, as it has now been revealed by the Spirit to His holy apostles and prophets:

[6] that the Gentiles should be fellow heirs, of the same body, and partakers of His promise in Christ through the gospel,

[7] of which I became a minister according to the gift of the grace of God given to me by the effective working of His power.

[8] To me, who am less than the least of all the saints, this grace was given, that I should preach among the Gentiles the unsearchable riches of Christ,

[9] and to make all see what is the fellowship of the mystery, which from the beginning of the ages has been hidden in God who created all things through Jesus Christ;

[10] to the intent that now the manifold wisdom of God might be made known by the church to the principalities and powers in the heavenly places,

[11] according to the eternal purpose which He accomplished in Christ Jesus our Lord,

¹² in whom we have boldness and access with confidence through faith in Him.

¹³ Therefore I ask that you do not lose heart at my tribulations for you, which is your glory.

Out of God's Word...

As you begin, realize Paul starts a thought in verse 1. However, when he comes to the words "you Gentiles," he digresses to explain more fully his ministry to the Gentiles. In verse 14 Paul will complete his thought from verse 1.

1. Begin by reading verses 1-5. Right away, what does Paul relate about himself (verse 1)? *He loves & believe in Christ as Gods son.*

   What had God entrusted to Paul, and why (verse 2)? *He was shown so He could record & tell it*

   The mystery was important to Paul and his ministry to the Gentiles. What does he say about it in...

   ...verse 3? *It was made Known to him so he could record & tell it —*

   ...verse 4? *So we can understand His insite to Christ*

   ...verse 5? *It was revealed in Gods timing not people*

2. Now read verses 6-8. What does Paul reveal about the mystery in verse 6? (Keep in mind this verse unveils what the mystery of Christ is.) *We all share in our love for off Christ & believe*

How does Paul refer to himself in verse 7, and to what does he attribute it? *It was given to him so he could tell it to others*

How does Paul describe himself and his ministry in verse 8? *He didn't feel worthy of this information but accepted it*

3. Read verses 9-10. At what point in time did the mystery begin (verse 9)? *In God's time*

What is one purpose of God's unification of Jews and Gentiles into one body, the church (verse 10)? *to unify all who believe in Christ*

4. Read verses 11-13. What do you learn in verse 11 about God's purpose and the accomplishment of it? *He made it known thru Christ & not until then*

What blessings do Christians enjoy as heirs and partakers of God's promise in Christ (verse 12)? *We can come to God & ask for anything & He will hear*

What does Paul reveal about his personal situation in verse 13, and what does he ask of his readers? *Don't be discouraged about what happened to Paul*

...and into Your Heart

- *The ministry of Paul*—Like Paul, you have been given a sacred responsibility from Jesus to preach His message. What specifically are you doing with this stewardship, and how can you improve? *Showed teach (gave it up a couple years ago) Remember people in prayer*

- *The mystery of Christ*—God's message through Paul is
that all barriers have been abolished by Christ. What
are you and your local church doing today to live out
the mystery of Christ, the breaking down of barriers
between races, ethnic groups, and social classes?

*our door is open on Sun. + we enjoy
sharing our lessons — we have Thurs afternoon
Bible study have several churches represented*

- *The ministry of Christ*—Every believer in Christ has
bold access to God's throne of grace at any time. Read
Hebrews 4:14-16. Pinpoint your needs today and bring
them before God's throne of grace. *Strength + courage
to do what I need to do*

Heart Response

Have you heard of the Rosetta stone, an archaeological
artifact that enlightened our knowledge and understanding
of ancient history? It is a basalt stone dating from 196 B.C. that
was found at Rosetta, a harbor on the Mediterranean coast
of Egypt. On a thrilling trip with my husband and a group
of seminary students, our tour stopped in London on our
way to Israel. The Rosetta stone was there in the British
Museum, and it bears parallel inscriptions in both Greek and
ancient Egyptian. It became a key to deciphering mysterious
Egyptian writings that were previously untranslatable.

Well, my friend, here in Ephesians 3 something *far* greater
is unveiled than the understanding of human language! Here
we have heavenly language revealing a heavenly mystery

from God. It is the key to understanding what God promised in the Old Testament—that all people would be blessed through Abraham (Exodus 12:3) and through Abraham's ultimate descendant, the Messiah, Jesus Christ.

Pause for a moment and give praise to the unchanging God that none of His promises will ever fail to be fulfilled, including the security of your salvation through His Son.

thank you Lord !!

*L*esson 10

Tapping into God's Resources

*H*ave you ever been in the presence of a person who prayed with great power? When my husband taught a class of senior citizens at church, there was just such a man in the group. On those Sundays when he prayed for the requests shared by others, we hushed immediately and focused fully on the genuine and impassioned words that were sure to flow from his heart.

Well, you and I had best hush ourselves now. The apostle Paul himself is about to bow his knees, head, heart, and soul before God Almighty and pray! As you will recall, he began to pray earlier (Ephesians 3:1), digressed in explaining the mystery of the Gentiles (3:2-13), and now returns to his prayer. Take note of exactly what it is Paul asks for on behalf of his beloved Ephesian friends and all believers in Christ.

Ephesians 3:14-21

14 For this reason I bow my knees to the Father of our Lord Jesus Christ,

15 from whom the whole family in heaven and earth is named,

16 that He would grant you, according to the riches of His glory, to be strengthened with might through His Spirit in the inner man,

17 that Christ may dwell in your hearts through faith; that you, being rooted and grounded in love,

18 may be able to comprehend with all the saints what is the width and length and depth and height—

19 to know the love of Christ which passes knowledge; that you may be filled with all the fullness of God.

20 Now to Him who is able to do exceedingly abundantly above all that we ask or think, according to the power that works in us,

21 to Him be glory in the church by Christ Jesus to all generations, forever and ever. Amen.

Out of God's Word...

1. *The resource of God's power*—Read verses 14-16. What does Paul pray for his readers in verse 16?

Too strength thru the Spirit

What more does he add in the first part of verse 17?

grounded in Love

2. *The resource of God's love*—Read verses 17-19. Regarding love, what is Paul's request in verse 17? *grounded in love of Christ thru the Holy Spirit*

   What does Paul desire for his brothers and sisters in Christ in verses 18-19?

   — *Comprehend the love*

   — *more than we can understand*

   — *filled with fulness of God*

3. Read verses 20-21. List the superlatives Paul strings together in verse 20 to describe God's ability to answer prayer. *what we need not necessarily what we want*

4. How does Paul wrap up his prayer in verse 21?
   glory of Christ forever & ever

...*and into Your Heart*

• *Your life in Christ*—Scan verses 14-19 again. Paul prayed for believers to be strengthened with might. For what do you need spiritual power and might today? *To able to go to Bible Study at Donna Gums*

How are you encouraged by the fact that you need only "comprehend" the power you already possess for the needs of today? *To pray + handle what comes my way*

Paul prayed for believers to be strengthened by the Spirit in the inner man. How does the Holy Spirit work in your life to empower you and help you become like Christ according to…

…Romans 8:26-27? *(Daily Bread 6-16-19)*
The work of the Spirit makes prayer work

…Ephesians 5:18? *Don't get drunk on wine But of the Spirit*

…Galatians 5:22-23? *All - thru love of Christ*

• *Paul's prayer life*—Paul's prayers for others centered on what God in His great love has done for His people through Christ. What does this reveal…

…about Paul's confidence in God's care for His own?
Thru faith + believe

…about his understanding of what is most important in a Christian's life?

What impresses you about Paul's prayer, and why?
The Consistency of required love of Christ thru the Holy Spirit

Which of his requests would you want made for you today, and why? *patience + Be able to attend the Wim Bible study*

- *Your prayer life*—How does Paul's heart and prayer instruct you in your prayers for others? *Remember them before myself*

In a few sentences describe your prayer life—how often you pray, who you pray for, and what you generally ask for yourself and for others. Then jot down some ways you can change or improve your prayer life.

How can you make prayer a higher priority? List several practical solutions.

Heart Response

Do you remember where Paul is as he prays for his friends? He's in prison, which makes these verses one of Paul's "prison prayers." As he sits in Rome under house arrest (he can receive guests but cannot leave his residence), amazingly Paul is not thinking about himself, but of others! As he waits for a verdict, he wonders about his dear friends in

Christ who reside in Ephesus. Paul acknowledges that he is suffering (verse 13), probably from physical difficulties and deprivations due to his many years of hardship, persecution, and multiple imprisonments during his ministry for the cause of Christ. And yet over the decades of that turbulent ministry, he had learned one vital lesson: to focus his attention on his spiritual blessings and resources—on God's strength and might, on the love of Christ—instead of his physical pain and needs.

Thus this prayer!

Paul's message to you is the same as it was to those in the Ephesian church. No matter what difficulties you face, no matter what you are enduring right this minute, no matter how bleak the future appears, no matter what your pain of body or soul, always look up. Focus on God through prayer and count your real blessings—the love of God and His power at work, strengthening you from the inside out.

$\mathscr{L}$esson 11

Living Up to Your Calling

Ephesians 4:1-6

As a child I remember my parents saying to me and my three brothers, "With privilege comes responsibility." Later as a parent, I heard myself passing this wisdom on to my two daughters—"With privilege comes responsibility."

As you enter the second half of the book of Ephesians, you will hear Paul beginning to instruct you with this truth as well. Up to this point, Paul has dispensed facts and truths about your life of sin and darkness before Christ, what Christ did for you, and your new position in Him as a member of the household of God. Indeed you—and all Christians—have been abundantly blessed by God. And such blessing and privilege should evoke from you an overwhelming sense of responsibility. In fact, it demands it! Therefore Paul moves on to point out the duties and behaviors that should define your life in light of such blessings. Learn now about "the worthy walk" to which you are called. See now how God

means for you to live up to that calling and live out the grace
He has so marvelously bestowed upon you. ·

Ephesians 4:1-6

¹ I, therefore, the prisoner of the Lord, beseech
you to walk worthy of the calling with which
you were called,

² with all lowliness and gentleness, with longsuf-
fering, bearing with one another in love,

³ endeavoring to keep the unity of the Spirit in the
bond of peace.

⁴ There is one body and one Spirit, just as you
were called in one hope of your calling;

⁵ one Lord, one faith, one baptism;

⁶ one God and Father of all, who is above all, and
through all, and in you all.

Out of God's Word...

As you begin, note that in the word "therefore" (verse 1),
Paul's is referring his readers back to what he had written
earlier in the first three chapters. Once readers are reminded
of God's many blessings, Paul transitions from doctrine to
duty, from principles to practice, from our position in Christ
to our pursuits as followers of Christ.

1. You've seen it before, but how does Paul refer to himself
    in verse 1 (see also 3:1)?

    prisoner of the Lord

And what is his appeal to those to whom he is writing (verse 1)? *walk worthy of the calling*

2. The body of Christ is to be one of unity. What four attitudes in a believer does Paul say will help make this possible (verse 2)?

— *lowliness*

— *gentleness*

— *long suffering*

— *love each other*

What part are we to play that makes unity possible (verse 3)? *all peaceful*

3. Circle in the scriptures on page 68 the number of times Paul uses the word "one" in verses 4-6 and write them here. Then note what each "one" describes.

— *me* — *same spirit*

— *all* — *Bond of peace*

— *love* — *unity*

— *Bond of spirit*

...and into Your Heart

- Unity and oneness in a church and among believers doesn't just happen. It takes work! This section of Scripture is about having and nurturing the right attitudes— those that promote unity among Christians. Learn more about these four right attitudes now.

    —*Lowliness* is humility. How does Philippians 2:3-4 help your understanding of this Christian grace, and how does it prompt you to change?

    Think about others

    —*Gentleness* is meekness and describes one who is mild-spirited and self-controlled. What does Colossians 3:12 say you can do to grow in this godly quality? *Compassion & Kindness patience*

    —*Longsuffering* or long-tempered means a resolved patience and refers to the ability to endure discomfort without fighting back. What exhortation in 1 Thessalonians 5:14 instructs you in this godly trait?

    Help people in their needs

    —*Forbearance,* meaning the ability to handle the faults and failures of others and refusing to avenge wrongs, is extended out of a heart of love. How does 1 Corinthians 13:4 state this?

    patient, Kind, does not voost think of other people first

With these traits in mind, make a work list of ways you can promote and contribute to unity in your church and body of believers. For instance, "Say nothing more frequently when I disagree with someone," and "Pray for a gentle and quiet spirit when I am wronged."

Listen, love, share
pray from love not duty

Heart Response

God calls us "to walk worthy of the calling with which [we] were called." In other words, our daily conduct is to match up with our position in Christ, with the conduct of our Savior. In short, we are to be like Jesus.

We bear a great label—Christian—and have a great responsibility to live up to it. Supposedly one of the soldiers of Alexander the Great was called up to be court-martialed for desertion. "What's your name?" asked Alexander the Great, the commander of the Greek army. "Alexander," was the man's reply. "Then change your name or change your ways," said the emperor.

Our conduct is an advertisement for or against Jesus Christ. That's why unity in the body of Christ is so important. Jesus prayed that His disciples and the church today would be unified (John 17:20-23). Let's fulfill our Lord's prayer. May we, by the sustaining power of God's Spirit, work toward unity in the faith.

Lesson 12

Understanding Spiritual Growth

Ephesians 4:7-16

One recent Christmas I was asked by a group to share about my favorite Christmas gifts received over the years. Well, there was no doubt about #1. The gift of eternal life through Jesus Christ is the ultimate gift of all time! But on the practical side of life, I surprised myself by answering, "Electronics!"—not jewelry, vacations, clothes, not even chocolate! No, my computer and cell phone—even my dishwasher!—landed at the top of my list.

The best gifts are those that are useful, those that help you live a better life, reach your goals, and benefit others. And no one gives more perfect gifts than God Himself. Enjoy now viewing and understanding some of the gifts He has given to the church and to its members...including you!

Ephesians 4:7-16

⁷ But to each one of us grace was given according to the measure of Christ's gift.

⁸ Therefore He says: "When He is ascended on high, He led captivity captive, and gave gifts to men."

⁹ (Now this, "He ascended"—what does it mean but that he also first descended into the lower parts of the earth?

¹⁰ He who descended is also the One who ascended far above all the heavens, that He might fill all things.)

¹¹ And He Himself gave some to be apostles, some prophets, some evangelists, and some pastors and teachers,

¹² for the equipping of the saints for the work of ministry, for the edifying of the body of Christ,

¹³ till we all come to the unity of the faith and of the knowledge of the Son of God, to a perfect man, to the measure of the stature of the fullness of Christ;

¹⁴ that we should no longer be children, tossed to and fro and carried about with every wind of doctrine, by the trickery of men, in the cunning craftiness of deceitful plotting,

¹⁵ but, speaking the truth in love, may grow up in all things into Him who is the head—Christ—

¹⁶ from whom the whole body, joined and knit together by what every joint supplies, according to the effective working by which every part does its share, causes growth of the body for the edifying of itself in love.

Out of God's Word...

It's been a joy to learn what all believers have in common and the blessings God has given to each and every one of His children. And now it's time to focus on how believers differ.

1. Read verse 7. What has been given to each believer?

   grace

   What determined the portion each receives of this gift?

   what Christ gaves us

2. Read verses 8-10. As you read, also look at Psalm 68:18, noting how Christ is pictured as a conqueror marching to the gate and taking tribute, spoils, and captives from a fallen city. Ephesians 4:8-10 describes Jesus' crucifixion, resurrection, and ascension into heaven as Victor forevermore.

   Share briefly what you learn about Christ in...

   ...verse 9— *He came to earth + raised up back to God + Heaven*

   ...verse 10— *full filled script from Jeloaba*

2. Next examine verses 11-13.

   Verse 11—List the various "gifted men" Christ gave to the church.

   —*pastors*   —*evangelists*

   —*teachers*   —*profits*

Verse 12—What is the function of these gifted people, and to what ends? *To teach and show all branches of people*

Verse 13—In a few words, what is the time line given for the process described in verse 12? *Everyone will know of Christ*

3. In Ephesians 4 Paul focuses on the gifted men Christ has given to His body, His church. First, a few definitions:

Apostles—This term can refer to Jesus' 12 apostles, including Paul, or to "sent ones" such as Barnabas, Silas, Timothy, Titus, and others called apostles or "messengers of the church" (2 Corinthians 8:23). When both groups died off, they were never replaced.

Prophets—This group of gifted men had the ability to give revelation from God—revelation of a practical nature, as when Agabus, in Acts 11:27-28, speaks of a coming famine. This group too ceased as the church matured.

Evangelists—This group, both past and present, is gifted to proclaim God's good news of salvation in Jesus Christ. Philip, one of the deacons chosen in Acts 6, was later called "Philip the evangelist" (Acts 21:8).

Pastors and teachers—This combined title refers to a single man with two functions, that of pastor or shepherd, who is to also teach God's people. This group of men is still present with us. Pastor-teachers provide the central leadership in local churches today.

Service gifts—In other epistles Paul speaks of service gifts. Read Romans 12:4-8 and list the gifts named. Also note to whom these gifts were given (Romans 12:4-6):

prophecy ministry giving leadership

4. Read Ephesians 4:14-16 and the evidences of spiritual growth produced by the ministry of gifted men.

Stability—How is *stability* defined in verse 14?

to be faithful + teach

What metaphors does Paul use to give you word pictures of those who lack spiritual stability?

Believe what ever they are told

How are unstable Christians fooled and led astray?

Believing what ever they are told + not looking at scripture

Maturity—How is *maturity* described in verse 15?

Believe in love for Christ

Truthfulness—What is said about truthfulness in verse 15? Also, note what is to temper our truthfulness.

Continue to grow in faith

Cooperation—What words describe the body in verse 16?

growing + learning His word + love

What is the role of "every part" of the body, and what is the objective? *Believe with whole heart + love*

believe spiritual

....*and into Your Heart*

- As you think about this passage about spiritual growth, what did you learn about...

  ...your responsibility to grow in Christ?

  pray, love the Holy Trinity & believe use our gifts

  ...your responsibility to serve in your church?

  do whatever our talents are

  ...your responsibility to know the truth and avoid those who tell you differently? *Read the Bible & study & have friends in Christ*

  ...your appreciation for your pastor-teacher?

  listen, learn & support with love

  ...your role in unity in the body of Christ?

  follow Christs teaching

- What three things will you begin to do to promote your spiritual growth and usefulness in the church?

  — *use my own gifts given to me*

  —

  —

Heart Response

Whew! This is a lot to grasp! And I know this lesson has gotten quite long. But please remember these nutshell truths: One main purpose of the gifted men God has given to us is to prepare believers like you and me for a ministry of service to others in our churches. And the end goal? To produce spiritual growth and maturity furthering the unity of believers in the body of Christ.

What a marvelous plan! But it requires responsibility and a serious commitment on our parts to ensure our own spiritual growth and encourage the same in others. If you're discouraged or overwhelmed, please don't be! Spiritual growth and maturity is progressive. God doesn't expect you or me to be mature overnight. As with our physical growth, spiritual growth is a steady climb until you reach maturity. (And won't the reward be great when we reach the summit!)

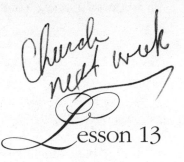

Carmen family service

Church next week

Lesson 13

Leaving the Old Life Behind

Ephesians 4:17-24

akeover TV programs are a big hit with female audiences. Maybe that's because we yearn for a second chance, a new beginning, a fresh start. For a sum of money, any woman can get a new look, hairdo, and wardrobe. But there is only one who is able to change someone from the inside out, to truly create a new person, to perfectly "make over" character, values, attitudes, perspectives, and motives. That, of course, is God. A Christian who possesses new life in Christ is different, set apart from the world, the temple of the Holy Spirit. Therefore a Christian should live in newness of life. Follow along as the process of spiritual growth is revealed beginning here and continuing through verse 9 in chapter 6. Let the Master's makeover begin!

Ephesians 4:17-24

[17] This I say, therefore, and testify in the Lord, that you should no longer walk as the rest of the Gentiles walk, in the futility of their mind,

[18] having their understanding darkened, being alienated from the life of God, because of the ignorance that is in them, because of the blindness of their heart;

[19] who, being past feeling, have given themselves over to lewdness, to work all uncleanness with greediness.

[20] But you have not so learned Christ,

[21] if indeed you have heard Him and have been taught by Him, as the truth is in Jesus:

[22] that you put off, concerning your former conduct, the old man which grows corrupt according to the deceitful lusts,

[23] and be renewed in the spirit of your mind,

[24] and that you put on the new man which was created according to God, in true righteousness and holiness.

Out of God's Word...

1. As you read verses 17-19, hear Paul's message about the difference that should distinguish a child of God from those who don't know God. Write out the admonition in verse 17. *Don't act like an unbeliever in Christ*

Review how the "walk" of the Gentiles (or unbelievers) is described in Ephesians 2:2. *lost*

How is the character of "the Gentiles" (those who are unsaved, who do not know Christ) described in verses 17-19? *ignorance of Christ (- not wanting to believe (not saved because of none belief)*

God is the teacher

2. Now for the great contrast that exists between believers and unbelievers! It begins with the word "but." Read it now in verses 20-24. What truth is stated in verse 20? (You may want to look at other Bible translations for clarity.)

How is one who has a relationship with Christ described in verse 21? Note too the facts about truth. *Heard + learned about Jesus from Him*

List the instructions for a whole new way of living as given in verses 22-24.

Verse 22— *Leave old life -*

Verse 23— *renewed by the spirit of my mind*

Verse 24— *live the life God wants from us*

Why must "the old man" be put off (verse 22)? *Former life*

How is "the new man" described (verse 24)?

what God wants from us love righteousness Holyness - Believe in God + Christ + Holy Spirit

...and into Your Heart

Paul says a relationship with Christ makes a difference in a heart—in your heart. Anyone connected with Christ seeks marked lifestyle changes. Paul first points out what the old man looked like and then describes the characteristics of the new man.

1. *The darkness of the old man* (verses 17-19). What is said regarding...

    ...the "mind" of an unbeliever (verse 17)?

    Futility of mind

    ...the "understanding" of an unbeliever (verse 18)?

    ignorance

    ...the "ignorance" of an unbeliever (verse 18)?

    blindness of Heart

    What kind of behavior does such a mind produce (verse 19)? *Greed- selfishness only believe in self*

    What do you think Paul wanted you to learn from this graphic description of the old man? *Make sure I've put it behind me + Believe in God, Christ + Holy Spirit (The Holy trinity)*

2. *The light of the new man* (verses 20-24). Paul now begins
   a description of the transition that takes place when a
   person comes to Christ, representing this new man as
   having "learned Christ" (verse 20). A believer doesn't just
   learn about Christ. He or she enters into an intimate, personal relationship with Him. Describe briefly how and
   when you "learned Christ" and embraced Him as Savior.

at less than a week old I was brought to Church by Mother + Grandmother. Got a way for me my faith + friend in Greeley asked if I'd like to go to Church with her -

To "put off" means to strip off and cast aside the old corrupt nature and replace it with the new life we have in
Christ. It's much like we take off and discard a dirty gar-
ment into the laundry basket and put on something fresh
and clean. A Christian acts differently. What do these
scriptures have to say about "putting on" a new nature
and conduct as a believer?

Galatians 5:16— *Live by the Spirit -*

Galatians 2:20— *Christ lives in me when I accepted Him + Savior -*

Galatians 5:22-23— *love, joy, peace, patience, Kindness, Goodness, self control*

Galatians 5:24— *Have left (crucified the old nature)*

2 Corinthians 5:17— *Spirit puts aside the nature + lets love, Kindness, caring be focus*

In light of putting off and putting on, do any behaviors, faults, shortcomings, or areas of sin pop up immediately in your mind? Also, do you see areas of spiritual change and growth that have occurred? Take a minute to answer both questions, making plans to change what is not righteous and holy, and giving thanks for what is.

Thankful for the Holy Trinities love & care of me & know when I die I will be in Heaven

Heart Response

The content in these packed verses calls for action, for change. Paul says, "You should no longer walk as the rest of the Gentiles walk." In other words, you (and I and all believers) are to stop living a purposeless life, to no longer live like unbelievers. They are dead in their trespasses and sins (Ephesians 2:1), but *you* have been miraculously raised from the dead! Therefore, do not live as the unsaved live, nor pattern your life after theirs.

It's quite a message, isn't it? And our response is to be an about-face. A 180-degree turnabout. A radical change. We are to decidedly leave behind the old self and the old life we knew before Christ.

Our heart response is also prescribed: We are to put off our former or old conduct, the way we lived before we belonged to Christ, and we are to be renewed in the spirit of our minds. One source explains leaving the old life behind this way:

> Living the Christian life is a process. Although we have a new nature, we don't automatically think all good thoughts and express all right attitudes. But if we keep listening to God, we will be changing all the time.[8]

Amen

Lesson 14

Changing Your Behavior

ears ago, when my husband was a pharmaceutical salesman, his manager would occasionally join him as he made his rounds to the doctors' offices. Jim's boss had been a top salesman before becoming a manager. He was so knowledgeable that he often spoke in generalities, assuming Jim knew what he meant. I'm sure you can imagine some of the challenges this created for Jim on the job. And I'm sure that you've had your own opportunities to be around people who speak in generalities. Well, thank the Lord, that's not the case with the apostle Paul. In this passage of scripture he is *very* specific about letting us know the ways we should act as we change our behavior and live our new morality as followers of Jesus Christ. There is no mistake about what Paul conveys that God desires for our behavior!

Ephesians 4:25-32

²⁵ Therefore, putting away lying, "Let each one of you speak truth with his neighbor," for we are members of one another,

²⁶ "Be angry, and do not sin": do not let the sun go down on your wrath,

²⁷ nor give place to the devil.

²⁸ Let him who stole steal no longer, but rather let him labor, working with his hands what is good, that he may have something to give him who has need.

²⁹ Let no corrupt word proceed out of your mouth, but what is good for necessary edification, that it may impart grace to the hearers.

³⁰ And do not grieve the Holy Spirit of God, by whom you were sealed for the day of redemption.

³¹ Let all bitterness, wrath, anger, clamor, and evil speaking be put away from you, with all malice.

³² And be kind to one another, tenderhearted, forgiving one another, even as God in Christ forgave you.

Out of God's Word...

In the previous section (4:20-24), Paul focused on the *fact* of a believer's new life in Christ. Here in verses 25-32 he shines the spotlight on the *behaviors* that absolutely must go...and those that should be added to this new life. Read them now and list as many instructions as you can find in these verses. Take your time and be thorough.

Negative behaviors to eliminate	*Positive behaviors to cultivate*
lying	work for others
anger	
stealing	forgiving
speech	Be Kind
feelings	to eachother
Bitterness	speak good words
	Take responsibility for my Sin
	edify the Church members

...and into Your Heart

Pretend you are walking through a photo or picture gallery lined with exquisite works of art. Instead of rushing through like so many people do, you choose to linger to study and appreciate each one. Take time now to look at the lineup of beautiful, positive behaviors God desires of you as portrayed in verses 25-32. What are His desires concerning...

Your honesty—Why and how are you to speak the truth (verse 25)?   *With Compassion*

Be sincere

Your emotions—What are the limits or guidelines regarding anger, and why (verses 26-27)? *Don't fight*
with others

What help does James 4:7 offer here?

Your work ethic—As a Christian, what attitude should you have toward work (verse 28)? *Help others in need*

What should your financial goals also include (verse 28)? You'll want to look at Romans 12:13 too. *Share*
Resist the devil & He will leave

Your speech—What kind of communication is out for you as a believer, and what kind is in (verse 29)?
Bad words spoken — Be considerate

What should be your goal when you communicate with others? *Listen to them then*
respond in love

Also, what does Philippians 4:8 say is key to the way you communicate with others?

pleasworthy & excellant

Your behavior—Have you ever thought about the Holy Spirit being saddened and grieved by the way you live (verse 30)? How does this motivate you to seek to live a more righteous and holy life? *To think more before saying something*

Your attitudes and actions—Which sins listed in verse 31 are areas of weakness for you?

How does the knowledge that these sins counteract the nature of Christ who lives in you (verse 30) motivate you in overcoming these attitudes and actions? *Remember to think before speaking*

How do these wrong attitudes and actions undermine the unity and edification (building up) of those in the church, the body of Christ? *hurts them & turns them away from accepting Christ*

Your relationships—How would the qualities and actions in verse 32 exemplify Christ in you and contribute to others in the church? *Use the talents I've been given for the good of Christ*

Which two or three commands hit you the hardest, and what will you do to "put off…the old man" and "put on the new man" (verses 22,24)?

pray more about situation

aware of the "old man" devil

Heart Response

Some scriptures call for a heart response of prayer, thanksgiving, humility, and inspiration. The gamut of reactions is great! But others call for action. I'm sure you know by now that when it comes to spiritual growth, you are not on autopilot. Nothing in the realm of spiritual growth comes automatically. You didn't instantly possess right attitudes or think right thoughts or make right decisions when you became a child of God. No, growth into God's likeness is a process, a day-by-day process. It requires a willingness to listen to God's Spirit as He prompts, convicts, and encourages. And glorious results are sure to follow! If you are obedient to follow His leading, you will be changing all the time from the inside—in your character, values, attitudes, perspectives, and motives. And, blessing upon blessings, these inner changes will be noticed as others see Jesus Christ reflected in your transformed behavior.

Safe travels to Casper Randi (Lisa)

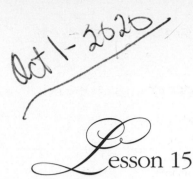

*L*esson 15

Imitating God

Ephesians 5:1-7

*R*ecently I received an e-mail from a mom who was writing to thank me for some principles I had shared in one of my books. She mentioned specifically how encouraged she was by the idea that it's never too early to begin training your children in the ways of God. Just that morning, as this mother was reading her Bible at her kitchen table, her little two-year-old daughter walked in with her children's Bible and crawled into the chair next to her mom and, opening her Bible, pretended to imitate her mom studying and reading her Bible. Never mind that the Bible was upside down!

Just as this little girl imitated her parent, we too should be imitators of God. How is this done? We imitate God by following His Son's example.

Ephesians 5:1-7

¹ Therefore be imitators of God as dear children.

² And walk in love, as Christ also has loved us and given Himself for us, an offering and a sacrifice to God for a sweet-smelling aroma.

³ But fornication and all uncleanness or covetousness, let it not even be named among you, as is fitting for saints;

⁴ neither filthiness, nor foolish talking, nor coarse jesting, which are not fitting, but rather giving of thanks.

⁵ For this you know, that no fornicator, unclean person, nor covetous man, who is an idolater, has any inheritance in the kingdom of Christ and God.

⁶ Let no one deceive you with empty words, for because of these things the wrath of God comes upon the sons of disobedience.

⁷ Therefore do not be partakers with them.

Out of God's Word...

1. As Paul writes, what does he urge of his readers in verse 1?

   The word "therefore" in verse 1 prompts the reader to look backward. Looking back to Ephesians 4:32, what kinds of actions qualify us to be imitators of Christ?

   Kind & tender Hearted

—

—

2. Paul continues. What does he instruct his readers to do in verse 2? *Walk in love*

Paul then points to Christ as our example of one who walked in love. How did Christ demonstrate love to us? *By coming to earth + dying on cross for us*

How did the Father reveal love according to Romans 5:8? *Christ died for us - (Before we werehim)*

3. In Ephesians 4:25-31, Paul described particular sins of speech and personal behavior. Now read Ephesians 5:3-4 and list several more actions that are unsuitable for believers.

— sexual morality   *— any kind of impurity*

— greed   *— Bad talk*

— obscenity   *— disobedience*

After giving this list of sinful actions, Paul refers to people who demonstrate these actions. How does he refer to these people in verse 5?

— No inheritance to heaven

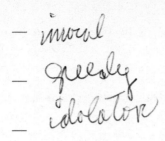

— *immoral*

— *greedy*

— *idolator*

According to Paul, what will be the consequence of their sinful behavior (verse 5)? *No inheritance in Heaven*

4. What warning does Paul give his readers in verse 6? *Don't be disobedient*

What does Paul say is true about the sons of disobedience? *No Heaven*

What command does Paul give his readers in verse 7? *Don't partner with them & their wickness*

...and into Your Heart

It's been said that imitation is the highest form of flattery. For a Christian, however, imitation is the highest form of love! Paul shows us how to follow God and show our love for Christ.

* *Walk in love*—How does Ephesians 2:2 describe your "walk" as an unbeliever? *Believed in people instead of Christ*

With salvation how are you to walk (Ephesians 2:10)? *To do good works*

How has your walk changed since you embraced Christ as Savior? *A peace that didn't have before*

- *Shun evil*—What are Paul's instructions in verse 3, and how serious does he consider sin to be? *By nature objects of wrath*

The Bible calls for not even a hint of sin in the lives of God's children! Sin is like a cancer which, if left unchecked, spreads throughout the whole body. It's like a spark of fire that can burn down an entire forest unless it is extinguished. Create a prayer list of any little—or big—sins you are holding on to that have the potential for disastrous consequences. How will you deal with them in light of Paul's command? *Don't care for some people*

- *Examine your relationships*—Paul warns there are some who say they are believers and rationalize their sinfulness. They even try to persuade others to participate in their sin. Paul orders Christians not to be deceived and not to enter into questionable practices. What do these verses say about relationships?

    Psalm 1:1—

    Proverbs 13:20—

Proverbs 22:24-25— *Don't be friends with people that are angry*

1 Corinthians 5:11— *Don't associate with wrong people & go their way*

1 Corinthians 15:33— *Don't be misled by wrong people*

Are there any people in your close circle who are dragging you back into the actions of the "old man"? What changes do you need to make in the area of friendships?

Chavel for Carmen Socotello

Heart Response

Modeling is a fact of human nature. That's why, whether you like it or not, you sometimes realize you're behaving much like your mother or father acted when you were growing up. Behavioral scientists call this "imprinting." Your closeness to others for any length of time leaves a behavioral impression on you. Therefore Paul is admonishing you and all believers to walk so close to your Savior that His way of life becomes your way of life, and His acts of self-sacrificing love become the same caring acts you perform in your love-walk through life. How can you be transformed into His image? How can you become an imitator of God? Read your Bible. Study the Gospels. Pray. Deal with sin quickly. Avoid ungodly people. And love God with all your heart!

Lesson 16

Reflecting God's Light

im and I celebrated a recent anniversary on the Big Island of Hawaii, which included a trip to the famous active Kilauea Volcano. We were told to arrive at the lava flow just before dark so that we could witness the most active area of hot lava at night. We were also warned to bring flashlights so we wouldn't fall while hiking in the dark.

As the sun began to slip into the Pacific, we started our trek over mounds of past-hardened lava. Right away we met a couple struggling to make the same walk without flashlights. Since we had two lights, we decided to give them one of ours. I can't imagine what might have happened if we hadn't come along with that extra flashlight.

In this passage the apostle Paul talks about the same need for light…but in the spiritual realm. Before we belonged to Christ, we were like that couple trying to walk on the dark path, stumbling and falling without the help of any light. But now we have the light of Christ in our lives! And God expects us to "let our light shine," to pass on the light, and to be a positive influence to those in darkness. What does it mean to walk in the light?

Ephesians 5:8-14

⁸ For you were once darkness, but now you are light in the Lord. Walk as children of light

⁹ (for the fruit of the Spirit is in all goodness, righteousness, and truth),

¹⁰ finding out what is acceptable to the Lord.

¹¹ And have no fellowship with the unfruitful works of darkness, but rather expose them.

¹² For it is shameful even to speak of those things which are done by them in secret.

¹³ But all things that are exposed are made manifest by the light, for whatever makes manifest is light.

¹⁴ Therefore He says: "Awake, you who sleep, arise from the dead, and Christ will give you light."

Out of God's Word...

1. Paul gives a description of the characteristics of one who walks in the light. To begin, what command is given in verse 8?

   A child of light walks by the Spirit. What characterizes the lifestyle of one who does so (verse 9)?

— *goodness*

— *righteousness*

— *Truth*

With what is a Christian concerned as he seeks direction (verse 10)? *live in light of Christ*

2. What is Paul's next command (verse 11)? *don't take part in evil but expose it*

And what does Paul add in verse 12? *Don't talk about it*

3. According to verse 13, what power does light have? *good is light of Christ*

How does Paul appeal to his readers (verse 14)? *wake up & follow Christ.*

...and into Your Heart

- Reflect back to your life before Christ and generally describe what it was like to live in darkness.

Now describe the difference living in the light of Christ has made.

• Your desires and choices as one who walks in the light are governed by your prior determination to please God and not yourself. Each action you take should be prefaced by asking, "Will this be pleasing to my Lord?" If what you are considering will please God, then it's acceptable...which means doing otherwise is unacceptable! What does Romans 12:1-2 say is essential for determining what is acceptable to God? As you write out each answer, also write out one action you will take to make it true of you.

   Step 1 (verse 1)—

   Step 2 (verse 2)—

   Step 3 (verse 2)—

• In verse 14 "Paul is appealing to the Ephesians to wake up, stay alert, and realize the dangerous condition into which some of them had been slipping by listening to false teachings."[9] In what ways does his appeal apply to you and your habits?

   So continue to pray at nite + on working in App

Heart Response

Imagine! Just as Jim and I were able to physically assist a couple walking in the dark by giving them a flashlight, you are able to do the same spiritually as you reflect the light that is yours as a child of the light. Christ is no longer present on earth, but *you* reflect His light to those in darkness as you...

- bear the fruit of goodness, righteousness, and truthfulness
- seek to know God's will
- shun the unfruitful deeds of darkness
- expose evil by the sheer nature of the light of your righteous life *Hopefully*

This Bible study is titled *Understanding Your Blessings in Christ*. Hopefully by now you realize you are unbelievably blessed as a child of God! And as such, God has a word to you:

> *You are the light of the world. A city that is set on a hill cannot be hidden. Nor do they light a lamp and put it under a basket, but on a lamp-stand, and it gives light to all who are in the house. Let your light so shine before men, that they may see your good works and glorify your Father in heaven* (Matthew 5:14-16).

Lesson 17

Practicing Wise Living

Ephesians 5:15-18

ake a wish!" How often have you said or heard this statement on your birthday or that of one of your children while blowing out candles on a cake? God in essence made a similar statement to King Solomon thousands of years ago. In fact, God told Solomon he could have anything he wanted. Anything! That's right. Let's see...how about a new car, a new house, new clothes, a new...etc., etc. But you probably know the story—Solomon asked for wisdom, "an understanding heart to...discern good and evil" (1 Kings 3:9).

The next time you pray or "make a wish" (so to speak), follow Solomon's example. Don't waste your prayers on physical or earthly desires and needs. Instead, go for the biggest and best of all. Ask God for wisdom! Now follow along as Paul tells you about wisdom and practicing wise living.

Ephesians 5:15-18

¹⁵ See then that you walk circumspectly, not as fools but as wise,

¹⁶ redeeming the time, because the days are evil.

¹⁷ Therefore do not be unwise, but understand what the will of the Lord is.

¹⁸ And do not be drunk with wine, in which is dissipation; but be filled with the Spirit.

Out of God's Word...

1. Once again—for the seventh time—Paul uses the idea of walking to describe our day-by-day conduct. To get a more complete picture of your daily walk, review and note what you've learned about the concept of walking in these earlier verses in Ephesians:

   2:2— world

   2:10— in Christ

   4:1— use what you

   4:17—

   5:2— love

   5:8— children of love

2. Ephesians 5:15 states that we as Christians have only two choices regarding our daily walk. What are they?

3. As you read through verses 15-18, note how a wise person conducts him- or herself. Note both positives and negatives.

Verse 15— *fool or wise*

Verse 16— *don't waste time*

Verse 17— *what the Lord require*

Verse 18— *follow the spirit*

...and into Your Heart

As one who's been awakened from the dead and infused with light (verse 14), you have God's wisdom and prudence (1:8). So the question is not, "Do you *have* wisdom?" but "Do you *apply* the wisdom and discretion that you've been given?" Work your way through these marks of wisdom.

• *Wisdom walks carefully* (verse 15)—To walk "circumspectly" means to be meticulously careful about the life you lead. A fool is not one because of what he knows (his intellect). No, he's a fool because of how he acts (his behavior). Think of several things you already do or don't do that indicate you maintain a careful watch over your lifestyle. *pray + help*

Now share several things you can do to be even more careful. *read & pray more –*

- *Wisdom evaluates its time* (verse 16)—The word "time" has the idea of a fixed allotted season. By writing "*the time*" Paul refers to one's lifetime as a believer in the midst of an evil world. Christians are to be aware of the brevity of life and "redeem"—buy back—time from uselessness and spend it to make every minute count for eternity. How does James describe the brevity of life in James 4:14?

And how does James describe the result of failing to redeem time for useful service (James 4:17)?
sin if I don't love & help

Name several areas in which you can redeem some time for more fruitful and meaningful activities, and purpose to do so. *pray for wisdom before ym* *Read Bible*

- *Wisdom follows a standard* (verse 17)—Spiritual wisdom involves understanding God's plan for your life and applying that knowledge. What do the following scriptures teach about doing God's will?

1 Thessalonians 4:3— *If you do good*
Makes foolish people look wrong

1 Thessalonians 5:18—
Should silence the wicked.

1 Peter 2:15— *Submit to superiors*

God's standards are revealed in God's Word. His plan for your life is unfolded as you study His Word, apply it, and pray for wisdom. How can you improve on gaining greater knowledge and a better understanding of the Bible?

• *Wisdom lives under God's control* (verse 18)—Ephesus was the site of the great temple of Artemis, or Diana, one of the seven wonders of the ancient world. A part of the pagan "religious" practices of those who worshiped Diana was excessive drinking. This practice was alleged to give the participants special insights from their deities about how to live. By contrast, Paul tells his readers that a wise person doesn't need to be controlled by alcohol or anything else. Instead, wise living comes from being filled and controlled by God's Spirit, therefore acting according to God's direction. What are the behaviors of those who are *not* under the control of the Holy Spirit (Galatians 5:19-21)?

How do we act when we *are* under the control of the
Holy Spirit (Galatians 5:22-23)?

exhibit Joy & Kindness love
& joy

Heart Response

Paul's heart is full as he shares God's ultimate wisdom
and plan for you and every other believer—that you "be
filled with the Spirit" (verse 18)! Paul is not referring to the
Spirit's indwelling at salvation. He is rather giving a command for believers to live continually under the influence of
the Spirit. He is charging you and me to walk in wisdom as
we live moment by moment under the control and guidance
of the Spirit. What a difference that would make in your heart
and your conduct. In the priorities you set. In the way you
choose to use your time. Just think of living—really living—
God's will! Of living wisely! Here is some practical advice
written by one soul after meditating on Ephesians 5:15-18
and considering the use of time for eternity.

> Always carry something with you to fill the
> moments that would otherwise be spent in
> idleness...a little New Testament...a text—
> printed on a card—which you can memorize...
> or a notebook in which you jot down helpful
> suggestions or prayer requests. These are all
> good ways to "redeem the time" and make
> golden investments in eternity.[10]

Living by the Holy Spirit

Ephesians 5:18-21

*R*ecently I was visiting with my just-widowed sister-in-law. We were reminiscing through some of my brother's quips and sayings. He always had a slogan or motto or saying for every occasion. One of them I applied just today as I wondered where to shop for a particular item. His saying guided me: "The place to go is the place you know."

In this lesson we are not looking for a place to shop. We are looking for a way to live! And the apostle Paul has a guiding word for us for *all* of life: "Be filled with the Spirit." As children who walk in the light, we are also to be children who desire to live in the presence and under the influence of the Lord Jesus, letting His mind be our mind and His actions be our actions. "Be filled with the Spirit" is a command that becomes the driving force for the instructions Paul gives throughout the rest of the epistle.

Ephesians 5:18-21

¹⁸ And do not be drunk with wine, in which is dissipation; but be filled with the Spirit,

¹⁹ speaking to one another in psalms and hymns and spiritual songs, singing and making melody in your heart to the Lord,

²⁰ giving thanks always for all things to God the Father in the name of our Lord Jesus Christ,

²¹ submitting to one another in the fear of God.

Out of God's Word...

1. To review, recall that earlier in Ephesians Paul contrasted the "before and after" conduct of believers. In 5:8 he further contrasted those in darkness and those living in the light. Now, in another contrast, what does Paul command in verse 18?

   —

   —

2. List three major evidences of the Spirit's influence.

   Verse 19 (Note too the variety of ways this is done.)—
   praise

   Verse 20— *thanks to God*

How often?

For how many things?

To whom?

In whose name?

Verse 21—

    To whom?

    And with what attitude?

...and into Your Heart

A person who is under the influence of God's Spirit, who is Spirit-filled, will exhibit certain attitudes.

- *An attitude of joy and happiness*—In the early church much of the worship involved singing. Christians spoke words of encouragement through Old Testament *psalms* put to music, sang *hymns* of praise and *spiritual songs* of personal testimony. All were sung with great joy! It's interesting to note that church history reveals that each new revival and moving of the Spirit brought with it a fresh outburst of joyous singing. What do these verses say about the role of singing in the lives of the early Christians?

Acts 16:25— *pray & sing songs*

Colossians 3:16 (Just a note: "Let the word of Christ dwell in you richly" is another way of saying "be filled with the Spirit.")—

James 5:13—

Think about your pattern of worship during the past few weeks. What was your attitude and countenance as you prepared for worship and attended church services? How will you improve your joyous anticipation and participation in the future?

• *An attitude of thankfulness*—Those in the early church remembered their pagan past and constantly gave thanks for their salvation. They were faithful to recall their before and after stories! They were also aware of the opposition of the government and pagan societies to Christianity and continually gave thanks that they were in the hands of God.

Today most believers joyfully give thanks to God for the good things that happen in their lives. But Paul says we are to "give thanks *always* for *all* things." What does Psalm 34:1 say should be the pattern of our praise?

What do the following verses say merits your praise?

Philippians 4:6— *pray with thanksgiving*

1 Peter 4:12-13— *rejoice in all things & trial*

How would you rate your thankful spirit when it comes to setbacks, suffering, or disappointment?

• *An attitude of submission*—Humble submission is foundational in all our relationships, whether to the government or to others in our believing community. Submission to governing authorities is based on law and order. What command is issued in Ephesians 5:21, and what is it based on? *Submit to & obedience in all things*

Are there any exceptions to our submission? *Can't require someone else*

Just a note: "In the fear of God" means reverential awe, the attitude of a Spirit-filled believer who is amazed that the God of the universe indwells and gives him or her guidance for every action.

In the same way that the Lord Jesus was a humble, submissive servant to the Father, each believer should desire to follow in Christ's footsteps in every relationship. Note two or three ways you can be more submissive to others this week.

Heart Response

What Christian doesn't want to please God? It's a matter of the heart and a heart-condition. As Jesus said, "If you love me, keep My commandments" (John 14:15). How can you show your love for Christ? Paul gives you the answer: "Be filled with the Spirit." When you choose to walk in obedience to God's Word, His Spirit will empower you to...

—give praise out of a joyful heart,

—give thanks out of a grateful heart, and

—give honor to others out of a submissive heart.

next week

Lesson 19

Following God's Design for Marriage

Ephesians 5:22-33

arriage is not man's invention. No, it was all God's idea. In fact, marriage was the first institution God established after creating Adam and Eve. In them He formed the perfect team. Together they were told to rule the world. They were to be a unified and indivisible force. However, with the entrance of sin into the world, that team became fractured as each brought their self-interests into the marriage.

When Paul wrote Ephesians, the institution of marriage had fallen on hard times—not only in the Jewish community, but also in the Greek and Roman societies. By addressing marriage and the importance of being filled with the Holy Spirit in that relationship, Paul is presenting revolutionary information. And it's revolutionary for our world today too! Today marriage is again in peril, and Paul's message is just as important as it was some 2000 years ago. Read on as he presents radical but miracle-working advice for marriage.

Ephesians 5:22-33

22 Wives, submit to your own husbands, as to the Lord.

23 For the husband is head of the wife, as also Christ is head of the church; and He is the Savior of the body.

24 Therefore, just as the church is subject to Christ, so let the wives be to their own husbands in everything.

25 Husbands, love your wives, just as Christ also loved the church and gave Himself for her,

26 that He might sanctify and cleanse her with the washing of water by the word,

27 that He might present her to Himself a glorious church, not having spot or wrinkle or any such thing, but that she should be holy and without blemish.

28 So husbands ought to love their own wives as their own bodies; he who loves his wife loves himself.

29 For no one ever hated his own flesh, but nourishes and cherishes it, just as the Lord does the church.

30 For we are members of His body, of His flesh and of His bones.

31 "For this reason a man shall leave his father and mother and be joined to his wife, and the two shall become one flesh."

32 This is a great mystery, but I speak concerning Christ and the church.

33 Nevertheless let each one of you in particular so love his own wife as himself, and let the wife see that she respects her husband.

Out of God's Word...

1. Before we begin, look again at Ephesians 5:21. What does Paul say is expected of every Christian?
    fear of God love each other

2. Read verses 22-24. Here Paul branches out to show the role of submission (verse 21) in marriage. What instruction is given for wives (verse 22)? *love the Lord & husband*

    What is to be the...

    ...manner of her submission (verse 22)?
    do what is right for each other

    ...motive of her submission (verse 22)?
    I don't - if we can't do & agree we go our own way
    ...model for her submission (verse 23)?

3. Read verses 25-27. What instruction is given for husbands (verse 25)? *love their wife*

    What is the...

    ...model of his love (verse 25)? *as Christ loves us*

    ...manner of his love (verse 26)? *good words & love & praise*

    ...motive of his love (verse 27)? *Be Holy & without blemish or wrong*

4. Read verses 28-33. What analogy or imagery does Paul use to describe what a wife is to mean to a husband?

love spouse as Christ loves us

How does Paul explain the image in verse 32?

love spouse

What does Paul ask of wives in verse 33?

same

...and into Your Heart

The word "submit" is a combination of two words with a military background. It means "to line up, to get in order, to arrange, to rank beneath or under." As Christians we are to voluntarily arrange ourselves under one another as God commands...not over one another. What do you learn about this concept in...

...Philippians 2:3-4? *look at what others/ppl need before what I need*

...Philippians 2:5-8? *Christ gave up His life with God to help us daily*

• *Wives submit to husbands*—In a few words, summarize a wife's submission to her husband. *agree to discuss together ditions to be made*

If you are married, are there changes you need to make to better follow God's plan for you to be submissive to your husband? Note them here.

Paul switches from submission to "respects" in verse 33.
Look up *respect* in a dictionary and write out a definition
here. *regard or esteem*

If you are married, how does your understanding of submission and respect affect the way you respond to your
husband? Is any fine-tuning or adjustment needed?

we do not submit to one other
we will respect their opinion but et.
May not be mine

- *Husbands submit to Christ's example*—A husband is to
  submit to Paul's instructions to love his wife with the
  same love Christ has for His church. In a few words,
  summarize this love. *Caring about where she lives + how I*
  should treat Him

- *Everyone submits to one another*—Submission is in no
  way limited to wives and to the marriage relationship.
  Every believer, married or single, submits to others. What
  are among the areas in which submission is required of
  Christians?

  1 Peter 2:13-14— *do + agree with people of*
  authority

  1 Peter 2:18— *respect + follow the leaders*
  Chosen

  1 Peter 5:5— *agree + do what God wants*
  He dos not like proud people

  Hebrews 13:17— *obey + follow leaders*

Can you think of any changes in attitudes and actions you need to make right away in these areas of submission?

Heart Response

Marriage is often described as the union of two selfish sinners. Therein lies the problem! But God didn't intend for the marriage relationship to be this way. The fall of man into sin affected everything and every relationship, including marriage. That's a picture of paradise lost! But God has provided a solution for the marriage struggle—Jesus Christ. Ah, paradise regained!

As a Christian woman, you *cannot* make your husband love you, but you *can* do your part and love your husband by following the biblical pattern of submission and respect. Your role is not to be determined by "cause and effect" (for instance, if he treats me well, then I will love, respect, and honor him and submit to him). No, submission is to be "as to the Lord."

The next time your sin nature tugs at you to disrespect your husband or fail to follow him, think of your Lord. Jesus is your example. He willingly submitted to the Father's will not because He was forced to, but because He chose to, because of His love for the Father. God is asking you to respect and submit to your husband out of love and respect for God Himself. Your submission to your husband is actually your submission to your Lord. If you obey God's plan and follow Christ's example, you will be following God's design for your marriage—a perfect design!

Following God's Design for Family

One of the greatest areas of fear women struggle with is for their children. Moms worry about their precious children's health, safety, spiritual growth, and future. But if you think the issues of worry for kids today is great, realize that in the Roman world of Paul's day, life was even more perilous for children. But the rise of Christianity did much for the condition of women and the institution of marriage, and it may have done even more for children. The ancient world was merciless to sickly or deformed children. Also, any unwanted child could be left unattended for anyone to have, and such children were usually picked up by someone to sell as a slave or to be raised for the brothels of Rome. Plus Roman law gave the father absolute power over his family. If the father was a tyrant, his wife and children could be subjected to a lifetime of cruelty, deprivation, humiliation, and abuse.

As you begin a new lesson—and a new chapter in Ephesians—note that Paul, after addressing marriage relationships, now turns to the matter of children and parents and their roles in a Spirit-filled family.

Ephesians 6:1-4

¹ Children, obey your parents in the Lord, for this is right.

² "Honor your father and mother," which is the first commandment with promise:

³ "that it may be well with you and you may live long on the earth."

⁴ And you, fathers, do not provoke your children to wrath, but bring them up in the training and admonition of the Lord.

Out of God's Word...

1. *A child's responsibilities*—Read verses 1 and 2. What command does Paul give to children in verse 1?

   What is the overarching guideline for such behavior?

   Why are children to do so?

What are Paul's instructions in verse 2, and what additional information is added?

What similar command is found in Colossians 3:20?

As a point of information, parents are not the only ones to be honored. The Bible gives this same command to:

Slaves toward _____ (1 Timothy 6:1)

Husbands toward _____ (1 Peter 3:7)

Church members toward _____ (Romans 13:7)

Read Exodus 20:3-17. What commandment is given in verse 12, and what is its promise?[11]

2. *A child's reward*—What two rewards for respecting parents does Paul point out in verse 3?

—

—

3. *A parent's responsibility*—Paul also has a word for parents. What are they not to do (verse 4)?

What are they exhorted to do instead?

Just a note: Paul has been speaking to both parents up to this point. The word "fathers" can also refer to both parents (see Hebrews 11:23, where the same word is used of Moses' parents). Fathers were the dominant figure in the homes of Paul's day and, because of the brutal culture of that time, fathers were the parent most likely to use harsh discipline. But mothers are also capable of abusive behavior. Therefore, Ephesians 6:4 can apply to both parents.

...and into Your Heart

What about your children? If you have children, God has important work for you to do!

- According to verse 1, what are moms to expect from their children?

  In your dictionary, look up the definition for *obey* and write it here.

  Look up the definition for *honor* and write it here.

  What example does Jesus provide for children (see Luke 2:51)?

- According to verse 4, what are moms to do faithfully as they raise their children?

What do the following scriptures have to say about this process, and what is the general outcome of carrying this out?

Proverbs 22:6—

2 Timothy 3:15—

• According to verse 4, what is God's caution to you as a parent?

Look up the definition of *provoke* and write it here.

If you're a mom, put this caution from God at the top of your prayer page and be on the lookout for signs and ways you may be provoking your kids.

What steps can you (and your husband, if he's involved) take to better nurture and instruct your children? Here's one to get you started on your list: Make sure you encourage and praise each child at least as often as you reprimand or correct.

Just a note: It is the parents' sin if they "provoke" their children to anger, but it is the children's sin if they become angry in rebellion. The wise parent disciplines with love, which is required to properly train children. Love forms the foundation for raising children.

What about your parents? Though you may or may not have children, you definitely have parents. God has a word for you too!

- Read Exodus 20:12 again. What is your attitude toward *your* parents to be, regardless of your age and your life situation?

  Think of several things you can do today to fulfill your responsibility as a "child."

  —

  —

  If you are married, what should your attitude be toward your *husband's* parents?

- Think of several things you can do today to extend such an attitude to your in-laws.

  —

  —

Heart Response

If you're a mom, you already know motherhood places great responsibility on your shoulders! Generally, because of the amount of time you spend with your children each day compared to your husband, you are on the front line of parenthood. Your influence is great, but don't fail to include your husband in the parenting process. God means for both of you to be vitally involved. Make it a goal to work as a team with him in your parenting. And be on guard against your children pitting the two of you against each other. Seek to be united in your discipline, talking over any parenting differences in private. And make it a mutual goal not to provoke your children. Your children will respond to your unity and be grateful for it.

Dear mom, no role brings greater joy or blessing than that of being a parent. It is with love and a prayer for you—a mom after God's own heart!—that I share these principles that guided me during those active, hands-on, childraising years! Love your husband. Love your children. Trust God for His strength. Stand firm. Own your responsibility. And as always, seek the Lord's wisdom through prayer, His Word, your husband's input, and wise counsel from those who have gone before you.

Lesson 21

Following God's Design for the Workplace

Ephesians 6:5-9

One of the biggest changes I've witnessed in the Christian community in recent years is the increased number of working wives and moms. With this shift, Christian women now face two problems. Amazingly, the first was dealt with by the apostle Paul (lessons 19 and 20)—the responsibility of being a wife and mother. Now, in this lesson, Paul will address a woman's responsibility as a worker in the workplace.

Slavery has been a hideous blight on mankind since the beginning of recorded history. It was developed into a fine art by the Roman Empire. Slaves numbered in the millions and were used by all levels of government and society. It wasn't uncommon even for slaves to own slaves! With the spread of the gospel, many slaves and slave owners were becoming Christians. God used His servant Paul to give instructions on how these two groups should function toward each other. Hear now as he describes how Christians should respond to each other as fellow believers in the workplace. Discover God's principles for divine labor relations!

Ephesians 6:5-9

⁵ Bondservants, be obedient to those who are your masters according to the flesh, with fear and trembling, in sincerity of heart, as to Christ;

⁶ not with eyeservice, as men-pleasers, but as bondservants of Christ, doing the will of God from the heart,

⁷ with goodwill doing service, as to the Lord, and not to men,

⁸ knowing that whatever good anyone does, he will receive the same from the Lord, whether he is a slave or free.

⁹ And you, masters, do the same things to them, giving up threatening, knowing that your own Master also is in heaven, and there is no partiality with Him.

Out of God's Word...

1. *God's work ethic*—List how a Spirit-filled bondservant, slave, or employee is to work.

   Verse 5—He is to be _____.

Verse 5—He is to work with an attitude of
_____ and _____
in _____.

Verse 6—He is not to work superficially
as with _____,
pleasing _____.

Verse 7—Instead he is to work
with _____,
doing _____.

What should be the extent of a worker's obedience according to Colossians 3:22?

2. *God's reasons for a work ethic*—Now note the reasons God's servants are to have this ethic.

Verse 5—He works as to _____.

Verse 6—He works as a bondservant of _____,
doing the _____ of God
from the _____.

Verse 7—He does his service
as to the _____,
and not to _____ ___.

3. *God's reward*—According to verse 8, what is the bottom-line reward for a worker, slave or free, who does good?

4. *God's instructions for masters*—Paul continues to give balanced instruction on authority and submission. What groups were instructed in...

   ...Ephesians 5:22-23?

   ...Ephesians 6:1-4?

   Now what new group is addressed in verse 9? Also note the following:

   The instruction—

   The warning—

   The common reason for a Spirit-filled approach by both—

...and into Your Heart

- *Applying work principles today*—While slaves and masters are a thing of the past, God's work principles carry over to workers and employers today. Workers are to be obedient to their employers and work with fear and trembling with respect for the authority of their employers. What additional information does 1 Peter 2:18 add about how a worker is to respect his or her employer?

- *Motivation in the workplace today*—A Christian worker must see himself in the following ways:

  Verse 5—Being obedient to his employer as he would obey _____.

  Verse 6—Seeing his job as _____ for his life.

  Verse 7—Doing his work as to the _____.

  Verse 8—Knowing that his reward for a job well done will ultimately come from _____.

  Just a note: "Do the same things" (verse 9) means that masters should have the same concern for God's will and for their slaves as the slaves were expected to show toward God and them.

In Colossians 3:23, how does Paul sum up the attitude believers should have toward work?

- *Evaluating your work*—Where does today find you? If you are in the work force, are you a worker or employer? Are you self-employed or a stay-at-home woman? Whatever your situation, are there areas of performance on your job that must change, be eliminated, or be improved? Search your heart, conduct, and attitude. Then list steps you can take to make needed changes a reality and to better serve Christ...and your boss!

Each morning before you leave home, be sure to talk with God about your time at work. Ask for His help with a wrong attitude about your job, your work, or your boss. He's ready, willing, and able to help you follow His design for you in the workplace—a design that honors and glorifies Him and is a positive testimony for Christianity.

Heart Response

Ultimately, all work is done for and unto God. Therefore your labor needs to be a worthy offering to the Lord, whatever your vocation or position on the job and at home. Do you see your work—all work, wherever it is performed—as a holy offering to God? Maybe you don't want to be working a job at all, but as long as you do, work for God! Your attitude of serving the Lord can transform even the most menial of tasks into a magnificent sacrifice of love that will truly bring Him honor. And never forget or neglect your *greatest* work— that of being a godly woman and servant to the church, a wife, mom, and homemaker! Don't lose sight of the truth that the work you do at home is your greatest and most important service to God.

Preparing for Spiritual Warfare

Ephesians 6:10-13

Understanding Your Blessings in Christ. What a perfect title for our look at the book of Ephesians! It's rich. It's encouraging. And it's laden with information about who you are in Christ and what He has done for you as His child. Paul spent the first half of his letter describing our many spiritual blessings. Since then he's been letting us know that, having been blessed by a union with Christ, we have the opportunity to be a blessing to others as we live a Spirit-controlled life. But beware! Being spiritually blessed and blessing others comes with a price—spiritual war!

A true believer like you (I hope and pray!) who loves God and serves His people is a threat to Satan. Satan will do everything possible to get your focus off your Savior and your service to others. So Paul now begins to close his letter to the Ephesians with a warning about spiritual warfare and instructions for the battle. Pay attention while Paul shares the truth regarding your need for spiritual preparation so you are ready to fight and win the war.

Ephesians 6:10-13

[10] Finally, my brethren, be strong in the Lord and in the power of His might.

[11] Put on the whole armor of God, that you may be able to stand against the wiles of the devil.

[12] For we do not wrestle against flesh and blood, but against principalities, against powers, against the rulers of the darkness of this age, against spiritual hosts of wickedness in the heavenly places.

[13] Therefore take up the whole armor of God, that you may be able to withstand in the evil day, and having done all, to stand.

Out of God's Word...

1. *The charge*—Read verse 10. What is Paul's first word to his readers?

   Paul is standing like a general in front of his troops, giving a last word of admonition and motivation. Who is he giving the charge to?

   What is his call to his "troops"?

   Where is the strength for the battle derived?

—In the _____ and

—In the _____ of His might.

2. *The protection*—Read verse 11. What does Paul tell his fellow soldiers to do for their protection?

   For what reason?

   How are the devil's tactics described?

3. *The conflict*—Read verse 12. Here we learn that the conflict is not fought on a physical level with human opponents (flesh and blood). Make a list of the believer's spiritual opponents:

   —

   —

   —

   —

4. *The conclusion*—Read verse 13. As Paul begins his conclusion, what is his very first word?

Here Paul points his readers back to his previous instruction. Recall or look back at Paul's message in verses 10-12 and state it here in a few words.

Now back to verse 13. What does Paul call believers to do in order to prepare themselves for spiritual battle against Satan and his demons?

For what two purposes?

—

—

...and into Your Heart

- *The believer's enemy*—The first rule of warfare is to know your enemy! Paul says the battle you are in is a spiritual one, and the enemy you fight has great power. What more do these verses tell you about your enemy?

    Luke 11:15—

    2 Corinthians 4:4—

    1 Peter 5:8—

In a few words, what is the scope of your enemy's power, influence, and goal?

What new aspects about the power of your enemy have you learned from these scriptures? Or put another way, what do you now know about your enemy that you didn't previously know?

- *The believer's battle*—In Paul's day, to "wrestle" (Ephesians 6:12) did not always mean a friendly athletic competition. Sometimes, as here, it referred to a life-and-death struggle between two opponents. Paul knew that the struggle was not a game with Satan. He and his demons are in a life-and-death struggle against God and His children. How does knowing the seriousness of this struggle affect your thinking concerning the necessity of your preparation for the battle?

- *The believer's power*—Look again at Ephesians 6:10, then at Ephesians 1:19-20. The same power that raised Christ from the dead is yours today. How does this knowledge give you confidence as you enter into your own spiritual battles?

- *The believer's victory*—The victor on any battlefield, ancient or modern, is signified by whoever is left standing. Therefore, standing firm against the enemy without wavering or falling is every believer's goal. Of course, the ultimate victory has already been won by Jesus Christ at the cross. But the day-to-day skirmishes and victories require that you faithfully and purposefully put on God's full set of armor each day—each "evil day" (verse 13). These evil days began with the fall of man into sin and will continue until Christ returns to establish His righteous earthly kingdom. Think of some reasons Christians are not experiencing victories in daily life, and list them here.

Now, do any of these reasons apply to you? What will you do to equip yourself and prepare for battle today... and every day?

Heart Response

I've made my own list, which I can't resist sharing. As you read along, compare it to your list. I'm guessing we're probably on the same track!

- *We don't recognize the danger.* We consistently underestimate the power of Satan.

- *We don't understand the importance of the armor God provides.* Maybe that's because we don't know enough about it. Good news! More information about this is coming in the next lesson.

- *We don't take to heart the fact that we are in a spiritual battle.* Therefore we must gear up spiritually. Without preparation and training, no soldier is ready for battle...including you and me!

- *We fail to realize we are constantly in a battle zone.* No, we're not merely in a mall, or an office, or a school, or even a house or apartment. Everywhere we are is Satan's territory, so we better be aware of it and ready, willing, and able to fight and go to war.

And speaking of standing up against the enemy, there's no reason why you shouldn't "be able to stand against the wiles of the devil" (verse 11). The victory is yours in Jesus Christ. Ask God to give you the resolve to "take up the whole armor of God, that you may be able to withstand in the evil day, and having done all, to stand" (verse 13).

Lesson 23

Putting On the Armor of God

Ephesians 6:14-17

*A*s a writer, it's amazing how what's happening around me shows up in my books! If I'm looking at the tide turn, an eagle soar, a stunning sunset, or a perfect reflection on a glassy lake, it somehow works its way into my writing. And we see the same thing occur in Paul's writing as he searches for words to warn and instruct his friends in Ephesus about the reality of spiritual warfare.

Think about Paul's environment while he pens this letter—he's a prisoner. For two years Paul has been observing Roman soldiers up close and personal. Day in and day out, he sits chained to the warriors who were charged with guarding him while he awaits an audience with Caesar, who will determine Paul's fate. Do you know what happened? Paul learned a lot about the soldiers' armor and weapons... and they learned a lot about Jesus Christ!

Ephesians 6:14-17

¹⁴ Stand therefore, having girded your waist with truth, having put on the breastplate of righteousness,

¹⁵ and having shod your feet with the preparation of the gospel of peace;

¹⁶ above all, taking the shield of faith with which you will be able to quench all the fiery darts of the wicked one.

¹⁷ And take the helmet of salvation, and the sword of the Spirit, which is the word of God;

Out of God's Word...

1. *The Christian's battle position*—Review by reading Ephesians 6:10-13 again. How many times does Paul call Christians to take a firm position in spiritual battle?

2. *The Christian's battle protection*—Now list and describe the six different pieces of armor mentioned in verses 14-17, along with any descriptive information.

   —

   —

   —

—

—

—

...and into Your Heart

As Paul begins closing his letter, he speaks of the struggle every believer faces every day. He explains it's not a flesh and blood struggle, but a great spiritual fight involving this world...and the whole universe. Praise God, the ultimate victory has been won by Christ. But what must *you* do each day to ensure victory in your stand against Satan?

Put on truth

Every soldier wore a sash or belt around the waist. Generally made of leather, it was used to tuck in any loose clothing during battle as well as to hold pieces of armor in place (such as the breastplate and the sheath for the sword). When a warrior was ready to fight, his belt was cinched tight.

Just as the belt formed the foundation for the armor, so *truth* is the foundation of the Christian's life. "Truth" in Ephesians 6:14 is either the truth of God's Word (John 17:17) or the idea of truthfulness (the believer's character as one who can be relied upon to know and share the truth). Whichever it is, the belt of truth is essential for doing battle against the lies, half-truths, and distortions of Satan.

- Read John 17:17 in your Bible. What is your daily plan for buckling on the truth of God's Word?

- Regarding truthfulness, what do Matthew 5:37 and Ephesians 4:15 say? What is your daily plan for polishing up this vital character quality?

Put on the breastplate of righteousness

The breastplate provided a soldier with protection from the neck to the thighs. No soldier would ever think of going into battle without his breastplate. For you as a believer, righteousness is holiness, and your faithful obedience to Christ forms a protective covering, a breastplate. However, the opposite is also true—a lack of holiness, or unconfessed sin, can leave you vulnerable and unprotected.

- Look at 1 Corinthians 11:27-30. What did Paul say about those who are involved in any form of continual sin?

- Look specifically at verses 28 and 31. What does Paul say ensures your breastplate stays intact?

    —

    —

Put on the gospel of peace

A Roman soldier had special sandals made of soft leather with studded soles that allowed him to hold his ground in hand-to-hand combat. Yet these shoes were light enough for a warrior to cover great distances in a single march. With this in mind, Paul tells Christian "soldiers" (that's us!) to stand firm with the message of "the gospel of peace" between God and man. Putting on truth, like putting on shoes, enables you to stand your ground, and in this case, against Satan's lies about God and His relationship with you.

• What do these verses reveal about that relationship?

    Romans 5:1—

    2 Corinthians 5:17-19—

    Colossians 1:20—

• How would remembering these truths give you confidence when Satan tempts you to doubt the peace that exists between you and God?

Pick up the shield of faith

Paul says "above all" (meaning "in addition to"), be sure to take up the shield of faith. Roman shields were made in two sizes. The shield spoken of here is the larger shield— 4½' by 2½'—designed for full protection. A soldier could set it upon the ground and crouch behind it as flaming arrows were aimed at him.

Faith. The term means trusting and believing God. It is the bottom line for Christianity and is involved in everything we hold to and have confidence in. The only way to "quench all the fiery darts of the wicked one" and thwart temptation is to believe God and His Word.

- What do these verses say about faith in God?

    Hebrews 11:6—

    1 Peter 5:8-9—

    1 John 5:4—

- Satan's fiery darts are indeed flying! List several ways to strengthen your trust in the Lord.

Pick up the helmet of salvation

The helmet was the next-to-last piece of armor that a soldier would put on. It protected his head from arrows and sword blows. "Salvation" is referring to the future aspect of salvation, not the past aspect of being saved, nor the present aspect of sanctification. Paul is writing about our future glorification, eternal life, and heaven. The helmet of salvation gives you confidence that a great and glorious victory is coming.

- How does Paul refer to the helmet in 1 Thessalonians 5:8?

- What do these verses say about your assurance of a future hope?

    Romans 8:38-39—

    Philippians 1:6—

Jude 1—

Jude 24—

Psalm 23:6—

- How should these truths help you when Satan attacks you with doubts about your future?

Pick up the sword of the Spirit

The sword spoken of here was used in hand-to-hand combat. This spiritual weapon has its origin in the Spirit of God, who teaches you what the Bible means and how to apply it.

- How powerful is the sword (Romans 1:16)?

- How insightful is the sword (Hebrews 4:12)?

- Bonus question: How did Jesus demonstrate the use of this sword in resisting temptation (Matthew 4:1-11)?

- If you don't know the Word, you can't defend yourself or use it as an offensive weapon in defending or sharing your faith in God with others. How can you grow to know more of God's Word?

Heart Response

Hopefully by now you realize you are engaged in a fierce spiritual battle. When you became a believer in Christ, you shifted sides, so to speak. You are no longer on the side of evil nor one of Satan's instruments of evil. You are a soldier in God's holy and righteous army. As such, God has given you a perfect set of armor that's just your size. With this armor you can win the daily struggles of living for Christ. But to be victorious, you must keep *all* the armor on at *all* times and be *always* vigilant for *all* sorts of attacks that may come at *any* time! Keep vigilant, Christian soldier!

> *Go onward, Christian soldier,*
> *as you're marching out the door.*
> *The battle must be fiercely fought,*
> *for victory calls for war.*

Lesson 24

Praying Always

*I*n several of my books I've mentioned that my husband, Jim, was in the Army Reserves for more than 20 years. He was never in actual combat, but every time he went off for training or on a call-up, the chances for harm to him increased. I didn't always know where he was or what he was doing, so the only thing I could do was pray for God's protection.

Here in Ephesians 6 the apostle Paul is down to his final comments. He's addressed the reality of spiritual warfare and the armor that must be used. By now we've learned quite a bit about Roman soldiers and their armor. But here's the final key to winning in battle: Ultimately, a Roman soldier's victory came from his strength in battle. His armor protected him from the blows of battle, but his physical power sustained him.

The Christian's armor, like that of a soldier, needs an outside power. In the Christian's case, the strength and power of God's Spirit infuses the armor through passionate, constant prayer. Paul began his letter by having us look upward...at our heavenly blessings in Jesus Christ (Ephesians 1:3). And now he ends it by asking us to look downward...at the blessings that come from praying on our knees.

Ephesians 6:18-20

¹⁸ praying always with all prayer and supplication in the Spirit, being watchful to this end with all perseverance and supplication for all the saints—

¹⁹ and for me, that utterance may be given to me, that I may open my mouth boldly to make known the mystery of the gospel,

²⁰ for which I am an ambassador in chains; that in it I may speak boldly, as I ought to speak.

Out of God's Word...

1. *Prayer for the battle*—List the four "always" and "alls" of our prayers that appear in verse 18:

   —

   —

   —

   —

What other elements are to be included in our prayers?

Praying always....

in _____

being _____

2. *Prayer for the leader*—What was Paul's prayer request for himself in verse 19?

Copy here your definition of Paul's meaning of "the mystery of the gospel" (see lesson 9, page 57).

What was Paul's prayer request for himself in verse 20?

How did Paul view his prison situation in verse 20?

...and into Your Heart

Sometimes a stay-at-home mom feels like she's on the sidelines when it comes to Christian ministry and even the battles that many Christians face "out there" in the working world. Then there are the homebound women who are forced to stay home for health reasons. Or the women who feel they don't have the gifts and abilities to be used of God. In all these cases and many more, you or the women I've described can have a global ministry. *How?* you wonder?

- *Through your prayers*—What formula does Paul give in verse 18 for this kind of prayer ministry whether you're out on the front lines or in service for the King of kings while stationed at home? See it now.

    — "Praying always" focuses on the *frequency* of prayer. What do these verses add regarding frequency?

      Romans 12:12—

      1 Thessalonians 5:17—

List any improvements you need to make.

    — "All prayer and supplication" focuses on the *variety* of ways to pray. Look up the word "supplication" and write out a definition. In your own words, what does supplication mean regarding your prayers?

    — "In the Spirit" focuses on the *force* of your prayers. As you line up your will with God's, your prayers possess the strength and power of the Holy Spirit. How does Paul affirm this in Romans 8:26 and 27?

    — "Being watchful" focuses on the *attitude* of your prayers. How does this prayer attitude fit with putting on the armor that Paul has been describing?

— "With all perseverance" focuses on the *resolve* of your prayers. Do you tend to pray only a few times for your prayer concerns, or do you persevere, storming the gates of heaven with your requests?

— "For all the saints" focuses on the *objects* of your prayers. Do you have a prayer list and are you faithful to pray for those who are on the list? How can you improve?

- *Through the prayers of others*—The great apostle Paul felt the need to have others pray for his ministry. You too should seek the prayers of others for your life issues and service. Who can you enlist to pray for you?

Heart Response

I wish I knew you personally, but even though I don't, I'm guessing you (like me) have many issues you must deal with—personal problems, worries, anxieties, temptations, and disappointments, not to mention other battles you are fighting. Your problems are real and your concerns are legitimate. But studies have shown that when a greater anxiety or concern comes along, the lesser ones fade away. Do you want to be free of your worries and anxieties? Then lose yourself in the real issues of life, the things that really matter, the spiritual battles that you and others face. Like Paul, pray always. Pray for others. Lose yourself in the spiritual needs of others through prayer. You'll discover that you cannot worry about yourself and pray for others at the same time! And pray for yourself—to be strong in the power of God's might.

Lesson 25

Thinking of Others
Ephesians 6:21-24

Everyone loves to receive a "Thinking of you" greeting card. In fact, I purchased a package of 35 cards just to keep on hand for encouraging those I know who are downhearted or suffering in some way. Here at the end of our wonderful study of Ephesians and the multitude of blessings that are ours in Christ, Paul is thinking of others.

As we've already learned, Ephesians was a general letter meant to be read in all the churches in the region around the city of Ephesus. That's why there are no references to specific people. However, as Paul closes his letter, he chooses to send it by the hands of a trusted friend who will bring his friends in Ephesus a more precise and personal greeting. As you read Paul's final words, it's evident that he is thinking of encouraging others, even while chained to a Roman guard and suffering.

Ephesians 6:21-24

²¹ But that you also may know my affairs and how I am doing, Tychicus, a beloved brother and faithful minister in the Lord, will make all things known to you;

²² whom I have sent to you for this very purpose, that you may know our affairs, and that he may comfort your hearts.

²³ Peace to the brethren, and love with faith, from God the Father and the Lord Jesus Christ.

²⁴ Grace be with all those who love our Lord Jesus Christ in sincerity. Amen.

Out of God's Word...

1. *God's messenger of blessing*—How is Tychicus described in verse 21?

   What was Tychicus' assignment (verses 21-22)?

   In the following scriptures, what additional information is revealed about the man Tychicus?

   Acts 20:4-6 (his origin)—

   2 Timothy 4:12 (his ministry)—

   Titus 3:12 (his ministry)—

Read Colossians 4:7-8. What additional words of description about Tychicus do you find in verse 7?

What was his assignment (verse 8)?

2. *God's minister of blessing*—Paul was a blessing to all who came in contact with him either from personal exposure or from reading his letters, and this epistle is no exception. He opens his letter to those in Ephesus by offering a blessing (1:3). Who was Paul blessing or praising?

What blessing was Paul acknowledging?

Who made this blessing possible?

3. *God's message of blessing*—Paul, God's minister, closes his letter with a benediction or blessing from God for his readers that reflects several of the themes in his letter. What are the two blessings he offers in chapter 6, verse 23?

—

—

What final blessing is in verse 24?

This final blessing comes with what two qualifiers?

—

—

...and into Your Heart

Paul returns to a general closing as he reminds the whole community of readers—"the brethren"—of three major blessings. In his benediction, he reviews some of the blessings found throughout this book of blessings. Paul then says that all these and many more blessings come to us from God the Father and our Lord Jesus Christ. As time permits, look at the scriptures that follow and try to summarize the major message or information in each one in a few words of your own.

- *Peace*—the peace of God and peace with God:

    1:2—

    2:14—

    2:15—

    2:17—

    4:3—

    6:15—

- *Love*—Love for God and love for God's people:

    1:15—

    4:2—

4:15—

4:16—

5:25—

5:28—

5:33—

- *Faith*—Faith in God and faith in God's people:

  1:15—

  2:8—

  3:12—

  3:17—

  4:5—

  4:13—

  6:16—

- *Grace*—God's unmerited love and favor:

1:6—

2:5—

2:7-8—

3:2—

4:7—

Put a star next to the blessings of peace, love, faith, and grace that ministered to your heart as you read them. Take a minute to briefly write out how these specific blessings have impacted your life. Then try your hand at writing a sincere prayer of thanksgiving to God for His many blessings to you in Christ.

Heart Response

Speaking from my own heart, it's been a wonderful experience to become better acquainted with some of the many and marvelous blessings that are ours in Christ Jesus...blessings from the very heights of heaven! It is incredible to realize that as children and daughters of the King, you and I have received *every spiritual blessing* (1:3). Believe it! There are no spiritual blessings missing! This fact alone should prompt us to fall to our knees in adoring praise.

But with such favored privilege comes responsibility. You and I are to live out these spiritual blessings in our daily walk with Godlike behavior. Thanks be to our heavenly Father that He has also blessed us with the power to do so through the Holy Spirit.

My friend, as you are obedient to God and rely on the power of the Spirit, you will experience the daily reality of your heavenly blessings in Christ as they manifest themselves in God's

> *peace* in your life circumstances,
> *love* that is unconditional and constant,
> *faith* that is strong and unswerving, and
> *grace* along with continued blessings.

*L*eading a Bible Study Discussion Group

What a privilege it is to lead a Bible study! And what joy and excitement await you as you delve into the Word of God and help others to discover its life-changing truths. If God has called you to lead a Bible study group, I know you'll be spending much time in prayer and planning and giving much thought to being an effective leader. I also know that taking the time to read through the following tips will help you to navigate the challenges of leading a Bible study discussion group and enjoying the effort and opportunity.

The Leader's Roles

As a Bible study group leader, you'll find your role changing back and forth from *expert* to *cheerleader* to *lover* to *referee* during the course of a session.

Since you're the leader, group members will look to you to be the *expert* guiding them through the material. So be well prepared. In fact, be over-prepared so that you know the material better than any group member does. Start your study early in the week and let its message simmer all week long. (You might even work several lessons ahead so that you have in mind the big picture and the overall direction of the study.) Be ready to share some additional gems that your group members wouldn't have discovered on their own. That extra insight from your study time—or that comment from a wise Bible teacher or scholar, that clever saying, that keen observation from another believer, and even an appropriate joke—adds an element of fun and keeps Bible study from becoming routine, monotonous, and dry.

Second, be ready to be the group's *cheerleader*. Your energy and enthusiasm for the task at hand can be contagious. It can also stimulate people to get more involved in their personal study as well as in the group discussion.

Third, be the *lover*, the one who shows a genuine concern for the members of the group. You're the one who will establish the atmosphere of the group. If you laugh and have fun, the group members will laugh and have fun. If you hug, they will hug. If you care, they will care. If you share, they will share. If you love, they will love. So pray every day to love the women God has placed in your group. Ask Him to show you how to love them with His love.

Finally, as the leader, you'll need to be the *referee* on occasion. That means making sure everyone has an equal opportunity to speak. That's easier to do when you operate under the assumption that every member of the group has something worthwhile to contribute. So, trusting that the Lord has taught each person during the week, act on that assumption.

Expert, cheerleader, lover, and referee—these four roles of the leader may make the task seem overwhelming. But that's not bad if it keeps you on your knees praying for your group.

A Good Start

Beginning on time, greeting people warmly, and opening in prayer gets the study off to a good start. Know what you want to have happen during your time together and make sure those things get done. That kind of order means comfort for those involved.

Establish a format and let the group members know what that format is. People appreciate being in a Bible study that focuses on the Bible. So keep the discussion on the topic and move the group through the questions. Tangents are often hard to avoid—and even harder to rein in. So be sure to focus on the answers to questions about the specific passage at hand. After all, the purpose of the group is Bible study!

Finally, as someone has accurately observed, "Personal growth is one of the by-products of any effective small group. This growth is achieved when people are recognized and accepted by others. The more friendliness, mutual trust, respect, and warmth exhibited, the more likely that the member will find pleasure in the group, and, too, the more likely she will work hard toward the accomplishment of the group's goals. The effective leader will strive to reinforce desirable traits" (source unknown).

A Dozen Helpful Tips

Here is a list of helpful suggestions for leading a Bible study discussion group:

1. Arrive early, ready to focus fully on others and give of yourself. If you have to do any last-minute preparation, review, re-grouping, or praying, do it in the car. Don't dash in, breathless, harried, late, still tweaking your plans.

2. Check out your meeting place in advance. Do you have everything you need—tables, enough chairs, a blackboard, hymnals if you plan to sing, coffee, etc.?

3. Greet each person warmly by name as she arrives. After all, you've been praying for these women all week long, so let each VIP know that you're glad she's arrived.

4. Use name tags for at least the first two or three weeks.

5. Start on time no matter what—even if only one person is there!

6. Develop a pleasant but firm opening statement. You might say, "This lesson was great! Let's get started so we

can enjoy all of it!" or "Let's pray before we begin our lesson."

7. Read the questions, but don't hesitate to reword them on occasion. Rather than reading an entire paragraph of instructions, for instance, you might say, "Question 1 asks us to list some ways that Christ displayed humility. Lisa, please share one way Christ displayed humility."

8. Summarize or paraphrase the answers given. Doing so will keep the discussion focused on the topic, eliminate digressions, help avoid or clear up any misunderstandings of the text, and keep each group member aware of what the others are saying.

9. Keep moving and don't add any of your own questions to the discussion time. It's important to get through the study guide questions. So if a cut-and-dried answer is called for, you don't need to comment with anything other than a "thank you." But when the question asks for an opinion or an application (for instance, "How can this truth help us in our marriages?" or "How do *you* find time for your quiet time?"), let all who want to contribute.

10. Affirm each person who contributes, especially if the contribution was very personal, painful to share, or a quiet person's rare statement. Make everyone who shares a hero by saying something like "Thank you for sharing that insight from your own life" or "We certainly appreciate what God has taught you. Thank you for letting us in on it."

11. Watch your watch, put a clock right in front of you, or consider using a timer. Pace the discussion so that you meet your cut-off time, especially if you want time to pray. Stop at the designated time even if you haven't finished the lesson. Remember that everyone has worked through the study once; you are simply going over it again.

12. End on time. You can only make friends with your group members by ending on time or even a little early! Besides, members of your group have the next item on their agenda to attend to—picking up children from the nursery, babysitter, or school; heading home to tend to matters there; running errands; getting to bed; or spending some time with their husbands. So let them out *on time!*

Five Common Problems

In any group, you can anticipate certain problems. Here are some common ones that can arise, along with helpful solutions:

1. *The incomplete lesson*—Right from the start, establish the policy that if someone has not done the lesson, it is best for her not to answer the questions. But do try to include her responses to questions that ask for opinions or experiences. Everyone can share some thoughts in reply to a question like, "Reflect on what you know about both athletic and spiritual training and then share what you consider to be the essential elements of training oneself in godliness."

2. *The gossip*—The Bible clearly states that gossiping is wrong, so you don't want to allow it in your group. Set a high and strict standard by saying, "I am not comfortable with this conversation," or "We [not *you*] are gossiping, ladies. Let's move on."

3. *The talkative member*—Here are three scenarios and some possible solutions for each.

   a. The problem talker may be talking because she has done her homework and is excited about something she has to share. She may also know more about the subject than the others and, if you cut her off, the rest of the group may suffer.

Solution: Respond with a comment like: "Sarah, you are making very valuable contributions. Let's see if we can get some reactions from the others," or "I know Sarah can answer this. She's really done her homework. How about some of the rest of you?"

b. The talkative member may be talking because she has *not* done her homework and wants to contribute, but she has no boundaries.

Solution: Establish at the first meeting that those who have not done the lesson do not contribute except on opinion or application questions. You may need to repeat this guideline at the beginning of each session.

c. The talkative member may want to be heard whether or not she has anything worthwhile to contribute.

Solution: After subtle reminders, be more direct, saying, "Betty, I know you would like to share your ideas, but let's give others a chance. I'll call on you later."

4. *The quiet member*—Here are two scenarios and possible solutions.

a. The quiet member wants the floor but somehow can't get the chance to share.

Solution: Clear the path for the quiet member by first watching for clues that she wants to speak (moving to the edge of her seat, looking as if she wants to speak, perhaps even starting to say something) and then saying, "Just a second. I think Chris wants to say something." Then, of course, make her a hero!

b. The quiet member simply doesn't want the floor.

Solution: "Chris, what answer do you have on question 2?" or "Chris, what do you think about…?" Usually after a shy person has contributed a few times, she will become more confident and more ready to share. Your role is to provide an opportunity where there is *no* risk of a wrong answer. But occasionally a group member will tell you that she would rather not be called on. Honor her request, but from time to time ask her privately if she feels ready to contribute to the group discussions.

In fact, give all your group members the right to pass. During your first meeting, explain that any time a group member does not care to share an answer, she may simply say, "I pass." You'll want to repeat this policy at the beginning of every group session.

5. *The wrong answer*—Never tell a group member that she has given a wrong answer, but at the same time never let a wrong answer go by.

> **SOLUTION:** Either ask if someone else has a different answer or ask additional questions that will cause the right answer to emerge. As the women get closer to the right answer, say, "We're getting warmer! Keep thinking! We're almost there!"

Learning from Experience

Immediately after each Bible study session, evaluate the group discussion time using this checklist. You may also want a member of your group (or an assistant or trainee or outside observer) to evaluate you periodically.

May God strengthen—and encourage!—you as you assist others in the discovery of His many wonderful truths.

Notes

1. Taken from Elizabeth George, *A Woman After God's Own Heart* (Eugene, OR: Harvest House Publishers, 2006), pp. 31-36.

2. Herbert Lockyer, *All the Books and Chapters of the Bible* (Grand Rapids, MI: Zondervan Publishing House, 1966), p. 265.

3. Many scholars believe the letter to Ephesus was a general letter sent to other churches in the surrounding area as well. Also, because of the many similarities between this epistle and Colossians, Paul may have written them about the same time. And, since Ephesus was near Colosse, Paul sends these letters by the hand of Tychicus, who along with the runaway slave Onesimus, are delivering Paul's letter to Philemon, Onesimus's master (Ephesians 6:21-22; Colossians 4:7-9).

4. Charles Hodge, as cited in *Search the Scriptures,* gen. ed. Alan M. Stibbs (Downers Grove, IL: InterVarsity Press, 1979), p. 218.

5. Lockyer, *All the Books and Chapters of the Bible,* p. 265.

6. William Hendriksen, *New Testament Commentary—Galatians, Ephesians, Philippians, Colossians, and Philemon* (Grand Rapids, MI: Baker Books, 2002), p. 133.

7. John Havlik, *People-Centered Evangelism* (Nashville: Broadman Press, 1971), p. 47.

8. Bruce B. Barton, ed., *Life Application Bible Commentary,* "Ephesians" (Wheaton, IL: Tyndale House, 1996), p. 88.

9. Barton, ed., *Life Application Bible Commentary,* "Ephesians," p. 107.

10. Richard W. DeHaan and Henry G. Bosch, *Our Daily Bread Favorites* (Grand Rapids, MI: Zondervan, 1982), January 2.

11. Most scholars resolve Paul's statement that Exodus 20:12 is the first command with a promise by explaining that verse 12 deals with human relationships while the command and promise in verse 4 addresses a person's relationship with God.

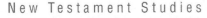

Books by Elizabeth George

- Beautiful in God's Eyes
- Breaking the Worry Habit…Forever
- Finding God's Path Through Your Trials
- Following God with All Your Heart
- The Heart of a Woman Who Prays
- Life Management for Busy Women
- Loving God with All Your Mind
- Loving God with All Your Mind DVD and Workbook
- A Mom After God's Own Heart
- A Mom After God's Own Heart Devotional
- Moments of Grace for a Woman's Heart
- One-Minute Inspiration for Women
- Quiet Confidence for a Woman's Heart
- Raising a Daughter After God's Own Heart
- The Remarkable Women of the Bible
- Small Changes for a Better Life
- Walking With the Women of the Bible
- A Wife After God's Own Heart
- A Woman After God's Own Heart®
- A Woman After God's Own Heart® Deluxe Edition
- A Woman After God's Own Heart®— Daily Devotional
- A Woman's Daily Walk with God
- A Woman's Guide to Making Right Choices
- A Woman's High Calling
- A Woman's Walk with God
- A Woman Who Reflects the Heart of Jesus
- A Young Woman After God's Own Heart
- A Young Woman After God's Own Heart— A Devotional
- A Young Woman's Guide to Prayer
- A Young Woman's Guide to Making Right Choices

Study Guides

- Beautiful in God's Eyes Growth & Study Guide
- Finding God's Path Through Your Trials Growth & Study Guide
- Following God with All Your Heart Growth & Study Guide
- Life Management for Busy Women Growth & Study Guide
- Loving God with All Your Mind Growth & Study Guide
- Loving God with All Your Mind Interactive Workbook
- A Mom After God's Own Heart Growth & Study Guide
- The Remarkable Women of the Bible Growth & Study Guide
- Small Changes for a Better Life Growth & Study Guide
- A Wife After God's Own Heart Growth & Study Guide
- A Woman After God's Own Heart® Growth & Study Guide
- A Woman's Call to Prayer Growth & Study Guide
- A Woman's High Calling Growth & Study Guide
- A Woman Who Reflects the Heart of Jesus Growth & Study Guide

Children's Books

- A Girl After God's Own Heart
- A Girl After God's Own Heart Devotional
- God's Wisdom for Little Girls
- A Little Girl After God's Own Heart

Books by Jim George

- 10 Minutes to Knowing the Men and Women of the Bible
- The Bare Bones Bible® Handbook
- The Bare Bones Bible® for Teens
- A Boy After God's Own Heart
- A Husband After God's Own Heart
- Know Your Bible from A to Z
- A Leader After God's Own Heart
- A Man After God's Own Heart
- A Man After God's Own Heart Devotional
- The Man Who Makes a Difference
- One-Minute Insights for Men
- A Young Man After God's Own Heart
- A Young Man's Guide to Making Right Choices

Books by Jim & Elizabeth George

- A Couple After God's Own Heart
- A Couple After God's Own Heart Interactive Workbook
- God's Wisdom for Little Boys
- A Little Boy After God's Own Heart

About the Author

Elizabeth George is a bestselling author and speaker whose passion is to teach the Bible in a way that changes women's lives. For information about Elizabeth's books or speaking ministry, to sign up for her mailings, or to share how God has used this book in your life, please contact Elizabeth at:

www.ElizabethGeorge.com